SPIRITUAL VITAMINS TO IGNITE YOUR FAITH

VOLUME 3

LEE MICHAELS

EDITED BY

NICOLE QUEEN

VISION PUBLISHING
HOUSE

Vision Publishing House

support@vision-publishinghouse.com

www.vision-publishinghouse.com

ISBN: 978-1-955297-99-8 (print)

LCCN: 2025922494

Unless otherwise indicated, Bible quotations are taken from the *King James Version* (KJV): KING JAMES VERSION, public domain.

This book is dedicated to the memory of my beloved mother, Fannie McCormick, and my dear son, Marques.

I honor the memory of my beloved mother, Fannie McCormick, who was there with me from the very beginning—nurturing, caring for, and most importantly, loving me unconditionally.

I also honor the memory of my son, Marques, who was taken from this life too soon, before he could experience the full beauty and promise it had to offer.

The memories of my mother and son, though for different reasons, keep my life and its focus in perspective.

But he answered and said, It is written, Man shall not live by bread alone, but by every word that proceedeth out of the mouth of God.

MATTHEW 4:4 (KJV)

CONTENTS

FOREWORD

As a personal friend and colleague of Rev. Dr. Lee Michaels, I am both honored and delighted to write the foreword for this newest volume in the *Spiritual Vitamins to Ignite Your Faith* series. These essential writings belong not only on our bookshelves and in our libraries—but also deep within our hearts.

In light of the sometimes rocky terrain, spiritual dehydration, and strongholds we encounter on our walk with Christ, these volumes are precisely what Heaven prescribes for our spiritual health and wellness. The Apostle Paul reminds us, "I press toward the mark for the prize of the high calling of God in Christ Jesus" (Philippians 3:14). Yet, this high calling can only be realized when we are grounded, rooted, and standing firm in our faith.

No conscientious Christian would deny that the Kingdom journey is often accompanied by heartache, tests, and trials. These trials can spill into our social lives, emotional well-being, church relationships, and even family dynamics. It's in those moments—when everything seems chaotic and we feel isolated—that the spiritual vitamins we have digested begin to elevate us, reviving our peace, purpose, and spiritual strength.

An anemic Christian—though sincere in their desire to glorify Christ—will inevitably grow weak if they are not spiritually nourished. Their stamina will be battle-tested. In this newest volume, Dr. Lee Michaels presents an indispensable and candid conversation on the believer's need to grow in grace, stay spiritually alive, and remain vigilant against the enemy's devices. His writing offers both an insightful analysis and a compelling call to action: reconnect with God, realign your heart, and reestablish your spiritual footing.

Drawing from decades of personal experience—as Pastor of Manifest Wonders Church and Performing Arts Center, longtime host of *Grace & Glory* TV, and former radio icon and program director at WCAO Heaven 600—Dr. Lee Michaels understands the soul's needs and vulnerabilities. It is reassuring when spiritual leaders not only discern these needs but also provide guidance rooted in compassion, wisdom, and practicality.

Staying connected to God is essential. So is recognizing when our spiritual tanks are running dry. Picking up these volumes and applying their truths will enable readers to run the race well, nourish their souls, and grow in grace.

Dr. Lee Michaels is warmly congratulated once again—as a pioneer who has offered the Body of Christ a vitamin boost that is actionable, practical, and deeply relevant.

Devon A. Blackwood
CEO, B.W. Associates
Professional Counselor, Author, Radio Host, Motivational Speaker
Doctoral Programs: Educational Leadership, Liberty University
Newburgh Theology and College of the Bible,
EdD in Christian Education

HOW TO USE THIS BOOK

This devotional is designed to guide you through a year of spiritual growth, reflection, and action. Each week features a unique theme based on scripture, followed by daily activities to help you apply the lessons to your life.

Here's how to get the most out of this devotional:

1. Start with the Weekly Devotion: At the beginning of each week, read the devotional carefully. Reflect on the central message, allowing God to speak to your heart through His Word.

2. Engage with Daily Activities: Each day, you'll find a specific activity to help you put the devotional's teachings into action. These may include reflection questions, prayers, outreach suggestions, or worship prompts. Take time to complete each activity thoughtfully, and let it challenge you to grow in your faith.

3. Use the Weekend for Reflection: The weekend activity is an opportunity for deeper reflection or shared experiences with family, friends, or a small group. These activities encourage community and allow you to discuss, reflect, and pray with others.

4. Journal Your Journey: Consider keeping a journal as you work through this book. Writing down your thoughts, prayers, and experiences each week will help you see how God is moving in your life over time.

5. Be Consistent: Growth takes time. Commit to reading and engaging with the devotional each week, even when life gets busy. Consistency in applying these lessons will help you strengthen your faith and your relationship with God.

Whether you're using this devotional individually or with others, it is a tool to help you grow spiritually, stay connected to God's Word, and live out your faith every day. As you journey through each week, remember that transformation happens one step at a time—so be patient with yourself and trust the process.

INTRODUCTION

Faith is not a one-time fix, it's a daily prescription. And just like our physical bodies need nourishment to stay strong, our spirits require consistent care and attention. That's the heart behind *Spiritual Vitamins* —a daily supplement of encouragement, wisdom, and truth designed to sustain you through every stage of your journey.

In this third volume, we go deeper into the rhythms of faith that strengthen our resolve and shape our character. Each devotional in this collection is rooted in Scripture and seasoned with real-life insight, continuing the legacy of spiritual encouragement that began years ago on my radio broadcast and now lives on through this four-part series. What started as a moment of inspiration has become a movement of motivation—empowering believers to face life's battles with boldness and joy.

By now, you've learned that life isn't always predictable. The unexpected comes, the storms roll in, and the weight of waiting can grow heavy. But through it all, God remains faithful. His Word remains true. And His promises remain intact. That's why this volume is filled with reminders to stand firm, press forward, and expect the victory that comes through faith.

Each page offers a new opportunity to center your day on God's truth—to shift your focus from fear to faith, from frustration to hope, and from weariness to renewed strength. As you read, reflect, and respond, may you find yourself not only encouraged but equipped to walk boldly into your next season with confidence.

You may be flawed, but you still have fruit. You may be waiting, but you still have worth. You may be wounded, but you still have a word. So take your daily dose because faith still works, God still speaks, and your story is still being written.

Let's keep growing. Let's keep going. And let's keep believing—one Spiritual Vitamin at a time.

FAITH THAT FINISHES STRONG

For we have become partakers of Christ, if we hold fast
the beginning of our confidence firm unto the end.

HEBREWS 3:14 (KJV)

"Faith got you started, but confidence will help you finish."

I engrossed myself in sports from an early age, and they became a
pathway of personal discovery for me in many regards. Growing
up in unfavorable circumstances and not having the kind of
influences in my life to encourage the winner in me, my means of
expression and discovery became sports.

I engrossed myself in football and baseball during those early
years, playing amateur sports at every level and opportunity. Later in
life, I developed a love and passion for basketball. Long before I ever
stood behind a mic or preached behind a pulpit, I could be found on a
basketball court competing, talking smack, strategizing, and getting a

good sweat on. As a matter of fact, looking back, I'm reminded that my broadcasting career began as a result of a destiny encounter after playing ball in my old neighborhood upon my separation from the Air Force.

Years later, once I started my broadcasting career, I formed a basketball team—first for WEBB, a station formerly owned by the late and legendary James Brown; then WBGR radio, the first 24-hour gospel radio station in Baltimore; and later at Heaven 600, where I served as Morning Show Host and Program Director for over 34 years. While we were passionate about the game, back then it was more than just wins and points. It was about identity. It was about legacy.

You see, that team wasn't just a group of guys running up and down the court. To the contrary, it was a brotherhood that took pride in what we stood for—as well as winning. Names like Freddie Lisbon, Rob Foster, "Squirrel," Mike Manns, Tyrone Whittenham, Glen Stanley, and Tidy weren't just teammates—they were extended family. We had a bond. We had a mission. And we had the confidence you could see before the game ever started.

We took on all challengers—church teams, military facilities, Job Corps Centers, government squads—and we even held our own up and down the East Coast in various tournaments. No matter the court, no matter the opponent, we played with something more than skill. We played with certainty, swagger, and the will to win. Why? Because we took pride in who we were and, more importantly, who we represented.

As a matter of fact, I'll never forget this one game in particular. There were only seconds left in the game. We were down by two points but had just seized a rebound and immediately called a time-out. With time not being on our side, we all knew we needed a miracle. But in the timeout huddle, one of our guys abruptly roared, "We're Heaven 600. We're gonna win this." And wouldn't you know it —we did, on a last-second three-point shot at the buzzer.

The takeaway from that experience and the answer to how we snatched victory out of the clutches of defeat was simple. We believed we could do it, even though the conditions suggested otherwise. We trusted each other. And we remembered that we were part of something special, a winning team with a legacy.

Now, shift that scene from hardwood to heaven. Hebrews 3:14 tells us that we are partakers of Christ—that means we're not just fans in the stands, we're on the roster. We are spiritually signed to a team that cannot and will not lose. But the condition is clear: we must hold on to the confidence we started with all the way to the end. In other words, never stop believing.

Understand that you didn't get drafted onto this team just to warm the bench. You're called to be a partaker, able to persevere in your faith journey. And to that end, you are called to be a participant on a team with a winning legacy—a team with a Captain who's never lost, a team where the victory was declared before the game even began.

But like any great team, there's a qualifier. You've got to stay committed in the crucible. You've got to hold on when the game gets tight, hold on when fatigue sets in, and hold on when doubt starts to whisper uncertainty. You've got to remember who you're playing for.

Many believers start strong—with fire in their soul and boldness in their step when things are going well. But somewhere along the way, when things get a little tight, confidence fades. Challenges come. Setbacks press. And the temptation to forfeit the fight becomes real. My word for you today is, don't give up the fight—hang in there.

Furthermore, I would suggest to you that this is when you have to reach back and recall the beginning—the moment Christ called your name, the faith that sparked your heart, and the belief that God was going to do something wonderful and great with your life. And let that refuel your faith.

You may not feel like the MVP right now. Maybe you're sitting on the sidelines of your own life, benched by disappointment, delay, or discouragement. But let me tell you something important: God's not done with you yet. You are still in the game, and as long as there's breath in your body and faith in your heart, you have a role to play and a victory to pursue.

Confidence in Christ is not cockiness; it's conviction. It's trusting that in the end you're going to win. Somehow, someway, you're going to win. God started it, and He's going to finish it. Philippians 1:6 echoes that very truth: "He who began a good work in you will carry it on to completion."

So don't lose your grip. Don't let your confidence collect dust in the locker room of yesterday's experiences. Just like our Heaven 600 team remembered in that moment of uncertainty who we were representing—so must you.

You're part of a team with an eternal record of redemption. You're walking with an undefeated Savior. And as long as you hold on, you're still in the game. That's the word I would like to leave you with— you're still in the game. I don't care if it appears that time is running out or if your circumstances do not seem good in the moment. You're still in the game—because of the team you are on.

And on this team, it's not about how you start, it's about how you finish. A faith that fizzles at the finish line isn't faith at all—it's hype. But a faith that endures all four quarters? That's championship-level belief. That's the kind of faith that wins the crown.

Proverbs 3:26 reminds us, "For the LORD will be your confidence and will keep your foot from being caught." In other words, you may trip, but you won't fall. You may be pressed, but you won't break. You may stumble under pressure, but God will keep you from going under.

Just remember: This is your moment to stay focused, stay faithful, and finish strong.

So tighten your laces. Step onto the court of your calling. Lace up your confidence. And listen for that voice of faith rising within you, reminding you of who you are and whose team you're on.

"You're going to win this." Because when Christ is your Captain, you always finish with the victory.

———

LIVING THE LESSON

Throughout the week, take time to put into practice what you've read and reflected on. Each daily activity offers an opportunity to deepen your faith and live out the lessons from this devotional. On the following pages, engage with these activities to grow spiritually and strengthen your relationship with God and others.

Monday | Scripture Focus & Reflection

Start the week by reflecting on your identity as a partner with Christ. Meditate on the following verses:

- Hebrews 3:14
- Proverbs 3:26
- Philippians 1:6

Reflection Questions:

- What does it mean to you to be a partaker of Christ?
- How has your confidence in God grown or wavered this year?
- What role does spiritual confidence play in overcoming adversity?

Journal Prompt:

Write about a time when you held on to your confidence in Christ during a difficult season. How did it impact your outcome? Reflect on how you can stay "in the game" spiritually, no matter the odds.

_____
_____
_____
_____
_____
_____
_____
_____
_____
_____
_____
_____

Tuesday | Personal Prayer & Petition

Spend today in prayer, asking God to strengthen your confidence in Him and help you never forget who you belong to.

Prayer Focus:

- Ask God to renew your boldness and courage to live as His representative.
- Thank Him for making you a part of His victorious team.
- Petition for discernment and resilience when you feel spiritually outnumbered.

Journal Prompt:

Write down anything God reveals to your heart during your prayer time. Where do you need to trust Him more? What has He already equipped you with that you may be underutilizing?

_____
_____
_____
_____
_____
_____
_____
_____
_____
_____
_____
_____
_____
_____
_____
_____
_____

Wednesday | Midweek Worship & Gratitude

Set aside time today to worship God for making you a part of His winning team. Let gratitude rise in your heart for the confidence He provides.

Worship Song Suggestions:

- "You Make Me Brave" – Amanda Cook
- "Confidence" – Sanctus Real
- "Do It Again" – Elevation Worship

Gratitude List:

- List three spiritual victories God has already helped you win.
- Write down a moment when God gave you boldness when you didn't feel strong.
- Thank Him for His presence and power working through you.

_____
_____
_____
_____
_____
_____
_____
_____
_____
_____
_____
_____
_____
_____

Thursday | Outreach & Encouragement

Encourage someone who may feel defeated or unsure of their spiritual strength. Remind them that they're still on God's team, and that He doesn't lose.

Outreach Ideas:

- Text or call someone who seems discouraged. Share Hebrews 3:14 with them.
- Post on social media a brief testimony of God's faithfulness.
- Write a note to someone on your ministry or church team and thank them for serving alongside you.

Journal Prompt:

How did encouraging someone else shift your own perspective on confidence and perseverance? What did you learn through speaking life to another person?

_____
_____
_____
_____
_____
_____
_____
_____
_____
_____
_____
_____
_____
_____
_____

Friday | Self-Examination & Recommitment

Reflect on your walk with God this week. Have you acted like you're on a winning team, or has discouragement taken the lead?

Reflection Questions:

- Have I relied on my confidence in God or my own strength this week?
- In what moments did I forget who I represent or what I carry in Christ?
- What do I need to recommit to so I stay spiritually locked in?

Journal Prompt:

Write down a personal recommitment statement. Declare who you are in Christ, and how you plan to finish strong, no matter how the game started.

_____

_____

_____

_____

_____

_____

_____

_____

_____

_____

_____

_____

_____

_____

_____

_____

Saturday & Sunday | Family Activity & Reflection

This weekend, spend time with family, friends, or a small group talking about what it means to "hold fast" to your faith.

Group Discussion Ideas:

- Share a time when confidence in God helped you win a spiritual battle.
- Discuss how families or communities can remind each other whose team they're on.
- Read Hebrews 3:14 together and talk about what "partakers of Christ" looks like in everyday life.

Weekend Reflection:

As a group, pray together for boldness, unity, and endurance. Encourage one another to stay rooted in Christ, especially when life feels overwhelming. Reflect on one shared commitment your family or group can make to walk in confidence this week.

_____
_____
_____
_____
_____
_____
_____
_____
_____
_____
_____
_____
_____
_____

DON'T IGNORE THE WARNING SIGNS

And the king of Israel sent to the place which the man of God told him and warned him of, and saved himself there, not once nor twice.

2 KINGS 6:10 (KJV)

"Every divine warning is a lifeline in disguise; obedience is your safest route."

Charles Swindoll once shared a chilling personal experience. He and his wife were flying from Portland to Los Angeles after a pastors' conference. Once the plane reached cruising altitude, meals were being served—but then the aircraft banked sharply. The flight attendants swiftly began removing trays and whispering among themselves. It was obvious something was wrong.

The pilot then came over the intercom, his voice steady and composed: "Good afternoon, ladies and gentlemen. We have a little mechanical difficulty. We're going to drop back in on the Portland airport. We'll be there for a little while, then we'll be back on course."

But the moment the plane landed, the urgency escalated. A flight attendant addressed the passengers: "Listen very carefully, everyone. As soon as we come to a stop, you'll hear a bell. At that moment, take the closest escape route you can. Some of you will go out the front, some out the tail, and we may even have to use the slide."

Then came the final warning that brought everything into focus: "There's a bomb threat. Take nothing with you—just get off!"

Would you believe it, despite the severity of the alert, some passengers hesitated. Others opened overhead bins to try to retrieve their belongings. All the while, the attendant kept shouting, "It's a bomb threat! Get off the plane!" Still, a few continued fumbling beneath their seats as if they were exempt from danger.

Isn't that just like us sometimes?

We're surrounded by warnings—clear, divine, even urgent—but we hesitate. We rationalize. We stall. We hold on to things that don't matter, risking everything just to keep our comfort.

What I have personally learned is that God's warning signs often come quietly, like a still, small voice. It could be:

- A lack of peace before an important decision.
- A recurring Scripture that won't leave your spirit.
- A sermon that speaks directly to your situation.
- A door that keeps closing, no matter how hard you try to force it open.
- A friend's honest concern that makes you uncomfortable but hits home.

Yet, like those passengers, many still ignore the signs. Some want more confirmation. Others want convenience. And many want to delay change—just a little longer.

But the truth is, God doesn't warn us to frighten us. He warns us to save us.

Still, obedience isn't always easy, but it is always worth it. The fact of the matter is, obedience and humility go hand in hand. It's been said that the first degree of humility is prompt obedience, and make no mistake about it, responding obediently to warning signs requires humility. One writer put it this way: "To reach the mountain of fame, one must go through the valley of humility." It requires trust—a trust that God sees what we don't, knows what we can't, and protects us before we ever know we need it.

Some struggle with warning signs because they can feel disruptive. They interfere with comfort, routines, and plans. But divine interruptions are often divine interventions in disguise. Moses was interrupted by the sight of a burning bush in Exodus 3, but as a result, he found a sense of purpose. The youthful Samuel heard a voice he mistook for Eli the High Priest, which revealed the call on his life in 1 Samuel 3. And of course, Saul, who at the time was on his way to persecute Christians on a Damascus road, eventually had his eyes opened to the truth that would lead to the transformation of Paul.

What am I saying to you? Simply this: God's warning signs may sometimes be disruptive, but they are that way by design to trouble the waters of your life and get you out of your comfort zone so that you can awaken to a sense of purpose, calling, and transformation in your life.

Others dismiss warnings because the threat isn't immediate. The skies are still blue. Everything seems calm. But ignoring the signs never delays the danger—it only removes your preparation. I'll say that again: ignoring the signs never delays the danger… it only takes away the opportunity to prepare.

I remember reading a story about a passionate mountain climber who set out to conquer a challenging peak despite a weather forecast predicting an approaching storm. Ignoring the ominous signs, other experienced climbers urging him to turn back, the unstable snow beneath his feet, and the distant rumble of avalanches, he pressed on, fueled by his animal desire to reach the summit.

As the storm arrived sooner than expected, visibility vanished and the treacherous conditions escalated, leaving him lost and in grave danger. Had he heeded the warnings, he could have turned back safely, found shelter, or planned for better weather, but now he stood unprepared for the conditions he had to face, all because he chose to ignore the warning signs, which only heightened the personal risk to him and removed any opportunity to prepare for the unforeseen challenges.

In the Desert of Judea, a voice cried out, "Prepare the way of the Lord." That was a divine warning, a spiritual announcement that change was coming.

In our Spiritual Vitamin, Elisha serves a similar role. Despite the corruption within the land and even within religious leadership, Elisha's ministry stood strong and faithful. He continued to hear from God, and he continued to speak what he heard.

And if I could, I would briefly pause here to say, sadly, it's a tragic commentary when the church—God's headquarters for light and truth —becomes polluted by the very darkness it's supposed to drive out.

We often recall the famous scene where Elisha and his servant are surrounded by Syrian soldiers. But before that moment came the build-up, which is the focus before us today. The king of Syria had been waging secret warfare—setting traps for the king of Israel. How many of you understand that the enemy is always setting traps?

Isaiah 59:19: "So shall they fear the name of the Lord from the west, and his glory from the rising of the sun. When the enemy shall come in like a flood, the Spirit of the Lord shall lift up a standard against him."

The "flood" imagery signifies sudden destruction, the kind of force that sweeps away everything in its path. It is a divine warning: danger is imminent when God's people turn from righteousness. Just as floods often come with warnings—rising waters, storm clouds, signs of impending disaster—so Isaiah alerts the people to the spiritual danger of unchecked sin.

A "standard" in ancient warfare was a banner or signal raised on high to rally the troops. When lifted, it warned soldiers of danger and guided them to safety or regrouping. In this context, the Spirit of the Lord raises His standard—acting as both a signal of warning and a defensive shield.

The standard reminds God's people: Do not ignore the signs. Do not mistake silence for safety. When danger comes, lift your eyes to the One who raises the banner.

In short, Isaiah 59:19 is both a divine warning signal and a promise of deliverance. It teaches us that when danger looms like a flood, God not only alerts His people but also lifts His banner of protection, ensuring that the flood does not have the final word.

The king of Syria was unsuccessful against God's people because every time he tried to "come upon them like a flood," God "raised a standard," i.e., revealed the strategy to Elisha. And every time, Elisha warned the king. And each and every time, the king adjusted—and avoided danger: "Not once, nor twice."

The lesson here is quite clear: the Holy Spirit still warns us today. He guides. He cautions. He redirects. And He keeps us from walking straight into the enemy's traps. What is required of us is to obey the warning signs just like He did with:

- The wise men, who were warned in a dream to avoid Herod (Matthew 2:12).
- Noah, who was warned of what was coming and built an ark (Hebrews 11:7).
- The Israelites, who were warned through Moses not to move without God (Numbers 14:42).

The devil knows your path. He sets traps. But God gives exit strategies—if you're willing to heed them. You can't expect victory if you keep walking past the signs and ignoring the still, small voice saying, "Stop. Reroute. Detour here."

So take a breath. Listen closely. And ask yourself honestly: Am I paying attention to the warning signs?

God doesn't repeat Himself without reason. If He's saying it again and again, it's because He's trying to rescue you from what you haven't yet seen. So don't ignore the warning signs.

LIVING THE LESSON

Throughout the week, take time to put into practice what you've read and reflected on. Each daily activity offers an opportunity to deepen your faith and live out the lessons from this devotional. On the following pages, engage with these activities to grow spiritually and strengthen your relationship with God and others.

Monday | Scripture Focus & Reflection

Begin your week reflecting on how God uses warnings to protect, prepare, and position us.

- 2 Kings 6:10
- Matthew 2:12
- Hebrews 11:7

Reflection Questions:

- How do you typically respond to warning signs—both natural and spiritual?
- Have you ever ignored a warning that led to unnecessary struggle or delay?
- How can you become more sensitive to the Holy Spirit's guidance?

Journal Prompt:

Write about a time when God warned you—through a sermon, a person, a dream, or a sense of inner conviction. What was the result when you obeyed or ignored that warning? Reflect on what that taught you about God's love and protection.

_____
_____
_____
_____
_____
_____
_____
_____
_____
_____

Tuesday | Personal Prayer & Petition

Set aside time to ask God for spiritual sensitivity and discernment to recognize and respond to His warnings.

Prayer Focus:

- Ask God to make you alert and attentive to His voice, especially in seasons of distraction or stress.
- Pray against spiritual deafness, stubbornness, or denial.
- Petition for the wisdom to take alternative paths when God redirects your steps.

Journal Prompt:

What warnings or red flags might God be revealing to you now in your relationships, health, spiritual walk, or daily decisions? Write a prayer of surrender, asking God to help you trust His direction, even if it's inconvenient or uncomfortable.

_____
_____
_____
_____
_____
_____
_____
_____
_____
_____
_____
_____
_____
_____
_____

Wednesday | Midweek Worship & Gratitude

Worship God for being a protector and divine navigator, One who never leaves us unaware.

Worship Song Suggestions:

- "Shepherd" – Todd Galberth
- "Lead Me" – Sanctus Real
- "Way Maker" – Sinach

Gratitude List:

- List 3 times God saved you from something you didn't even realize until later.
- Thank Him for the times He closed doors, disrupted plans, or caused delays that actually protected you.
- Write a praise declaration: *"God, I thank You for Your warnings, even when I didn't understand them at the time."*

_____
_____
_____
_____
_____
_____
_____
_____
_____
_____
_____
_____
_____
_____
_____
_____
_____

Thursday | Outreach & Encouragement

Take time today to lovingly warn or guide someone who may be heading down an unwise path.

Outreach Ideas:

- Call or message a friend who's facing a big decision. Ask them if they've prayed about it.
- Share 2 Kings 6:10 or a testimony of when God redirected your life.
- Encourage someone to seek God's guidance before they move forward, and offer to pray with them.

Journal Prompt:

How did it feel to lovingly warn or guide someone else? Were you hesitant? Did it reveal anything about your own sensitivity to correction or warning?

_____
_____
_____
_____
_____
_____
_____
_____
_____
_____
_____
_____
_____
_____
_____

Friday | Self-Examination & Recommitment

Today, reflect on how you've responded to God's warning signs in your life.

Reflection Questions:

- Have I been ignoring any spiritual warning signs lately?
- Is there anything God has been cautioning me about that I've been avoiding?
- Am I quick to obey when God speaks, or do I require multiple confirmations?

Journal Prompt:

Write a letter to God recommitting to obeying quickly when He speaks. Ask Him to soften your heart and give you a spirit that says "yes" the first time.

_____
_____
_____
_____
_____
_____
_____
_____
_____
_____
_____
_____
_____
_____
_____
_____
_____
_____

Saturday & Sunday | Family Activity & Reflection

Use the weekend to reflect with your family or small group on the importance of recognizing and responding to divine warnings.

Group Discussion Ideas:

- Have each person share a time when they sensed a warning from God. What was the outcome?
- Read 2 Kings 6:8–10 and Matthew 2:12 together. Discuss how God's warnings come in various ways.
- As a family or group, brainstorm how you can stay spiritually alert and accountable to one another.

Weekend Reflection:

Close in prayer together, asking God to protect your home, direct your paths, and speak clearly when you're in danger or going the wrong way. Commit as a family to follow His voice, even when it leads to unexpected places.

_____
_____
_____
_____
_____
_____
_____
_____
_____
_____
_____
_____
_____

BE THE MESSAGE

But we were gentle among you, even as a nurse cherisheth her children: So being affectionately desirous of you, we were willing to have imparted unto you, not the gospel of God only, but also our own souls, because ye were dear unto us.

1 THESSALONIANS 2:7–8

"Don't just pass on the message. Be the message."

H ave you ever received spam in your email inbox? You know the kind: messages that promise one thing in the subject line but deliver something entirely different in the body. Some are harmless ads, but others are dangerous scams.

They bait you with offers of inheritances, settlements, or packages waiting for delivery. "Click here," they say. "Confirm your identity. Verify your address. Claim what's yours." But instead of giving you what was promised, they steal what you already have.

Here's the deeper issue: the message claimed one thing, but the content didn't match. The subject line got your attention, but the body of the message betrayed your trust. Sadly, that's not just an email problem. That's a spiritual problem, too.

In our Spiritual Vitamin, the Apostle Paul praises the church in Thessalonica—not only for their faith but also for its authenticity. He's grateful not just that they received the message, but that they were living it. In other words, the subject line matched the body of the message he received about them.

He writes with tenderness and transparency, describing how he gave them not only the gospel but also his very self.

Paul understood something critical: The gospel is not just something we proclaim (subject line); it's something we embody (body of the message). In other words, the message of grace must be visible in the life of the messenger.

And this is where many fall short. They have a Christian "subject line," but a contradictory lifestyle. They talk about love but operate in judgment. They proclaim peace but stir division. They wear the title of "believer" but lack the substance of belief.

Proverbs 20:6 puts it this way: "Most men will proclaim each his own goodness, but who can find a faithful man? " We're quick to profess, but what we live often speaks louder than what we say.

Jesus put it bluntly in Matthew 7:23: "I never knew you. Depart from Me, you who practice lawlessness." That's a subject line with no substance—religious noise with no relational truth.

In contrast, Paul told Timothy in 1 Timothy 6:12: "Fight the good fight of faith… and confess the good confession in the presence of many witnesses."

It's interesting to note that he speaks of "fighting the good fight of faith," or the demonstration before the declaration, "confess the good confession," which reminded me that demonstration should precede declaration, because, as we have all heard, "actions speak louder than words." In other words, people should be able to see it in me before they hear it from me. But take note, Paul didn't stop at confession—he followed through with compassion. In 1 Corinthians 13, he reminded the church that even giftedness without love is noise: "I've become sounding brass or a clanging cymbal."

That's the warning: don't let your Christianity become spam, attention-grabbing but an empty message.

Paul authenticated his message by his lifestyle—by gentleness, sacrifice, and relationship. He didn't just show up. He showed love. He didn't just preach truth. He lived it. He wasn't aloof. He was available. He didn't just point the way. He walked it with them.

And according to our Spiritual Vitamin, He gave them two gifts: the gospel of God and His very soul. What a model for us today. Be the message. Don't just broadcast it, become it.

Here's your charge today: Don't just post it. Don't just preach it. Don't just proclaim it.

Be it. Let the content of your life validate the subject line of your faith. Let people see the gospel in how you nurture, how you sacrifice, how you serve, how you stay present—just as Paul said: "We were gentle among you, like a mother cherishing her children."

Be the message that doesn't just say God is love—but shows it. Remember, love is an action word; it is made visible by work.

Because in a world filled with noise and spiritual spam, the real message is the one that comes with a heart behind it.

So how do you "be the message"? You do it by practicing what you preach. When you say God forgives, forgive those who've wronged you. When you say God is patient, show patience in your relationships. When you say God restores, be an agent of restoration to someone broken.

Sometimes, the most powerful sermons aren't spoken—they're lived. Ask yourself this question on a daily basis: if someone followed you for a week with no context of your faith confession, would they still know you were a believer by your attitude, actions, and love?

Jesus was the ultimate example of being the message. He didn't just talk about love; He became love. He didn't just describe grace; He embodied it. He didn't just call for sacrifice; He offered Himself.

That's what it means to be the message. When your walk echoes your words, when your life affirms your lips, and when your faith shows up in your follow-through—you are the message.

So whether you're a pastor, a parent, a teacher, a leader, a friend, or simply someone trying to live right, remember that the loudest sermon is the one others witness in you daily.

Don't just talk the gospel. Live it. Don't just quote Scripture. Embody it. Don't just invite people to church. Bring the church to them through your actions.

You are a living letter—written not with ink, but with the Spirit of the living God.

So today, let your subject line be "Jesus," and let your body content be grace, truth, humility, and love.

Be the message.

LIVING THE LESSON

Throughout the week, take time to put into practice what you've read and reflected on. Each daily activity offers an opportunity to deepen your faith and live out the lessons from this devotional. On the following pages, engage with these activities to grow spiritually and strengthen your relationship with God and others.

Monday | Scripture Focus & Reflection

Start the week by meditating on how your lifestyle matches your message.

- 1 Thessalonians 2:7–8
- 1 Corinthians 13:1–3
- Matthew 7:21–23

Reflection Questions:

- In what areas of your life does your walk match your talk?
- Are there areas where your words and actions might be misaligned?
- How do you respond to people when they fail or disappoint you? Does it reflect Christ?

Journal Prompt:

Write about how your relationships reflect your faith. Are you living in a way that validates your testimony? Ask God to help you live as a clear, loving, and consistent message of His grace.

_____
_____
_____
_____
_____
_____
_____
_____
_____
_____
_____
_____
_____

Tuesday | Personal Prayer & Petition

Pray today for integrity, humility, and a heart that reflects the gospel in action, not just in words.

Prayer Focus:

- Ask God to reveal areas where your life doesn't fully reflect your confession of faith.
- Pray for the fruit of the Spirit to be evident in your relationships.
- Petition for the grace to love others well and be the message of Christ in everyday life.

Journal Prompt:

Write down what God reveals to you in prayer today. Are there relationships that need healing? Areas where you've been "all words and no substance"? Ask the Lord to transform those areas.

_____

_____

_____

_____

_____

_____

_____

_____

_____

_____

_____

_____

_____

_____

_____

Wednesday | Midweek Worship & Gratitude

Worship God for the privilege of carrying His message, and being transformed into His likeness.

Worship Song Suggestions:

- "Refiner" – Maverick City Music
- "More Like Jesus" – Passion
- "Build My Life" – Housefires

Gratitude List:

- Thank God for someone in your life who *lived* the gospel— not just preached it.
- Write down three character traits Jesus modeled that you want to develop more deeply.
- Thank God that He loves you *as you are,* and yet never stops refining you.

_____
_____
_____
_____
_____
_____
_____
_____
_____
_____
_____
_____
_____
_____
_____

Thursday | Outreach & Encouragement

Live out the message today. Find a way to *be the message* of grace, truth, and love in someone's life.

Outreach Ideas:

- Offer a listening ear to someone going through a difficult time.
- Write a note or send a text to someone who inspires you because their life matches their faith.
- Show up for someone today—not with words, but with presence.

Journal Prompt:

What did it feel like to be the message today? Did your actions speak louder than your words? Reflect on how your outreach impacted both you and the person you encouraged.

_____

_____

_____

_____

_____

_____

_____

_____

_____

_____

_____

_____

_____

_____

Friday | Self-Examination & Recommitment

Examine the ways you've lived—or failed to live—the message this week.

Reflection Questions:

- Have I loved unconditionally and generously this week?
- Did I say something that contradicted the love and patience of Christ?
- Am I being transformed or just talking about transformation?

Journaling Prompt:

Write a recommitment to "being the message" in your everyday life, especially with your family, coworkers, and community. Reflect on how you can offer *both* the gospel *and* your life to those around you.

_____

_____

_____

_____

_____

_____

_____

_____

_____

_____

_____

_____

_____

_____

_____

_____

_____

Saturday & Sunday | Family Activity & Reflection

Use this weekend to talk as a family or small group about what it looks like to "be the message."

Group Discussion Ideas:

- Share stories of people who didn't just talk about their faith but lived it out with love.
- Discuss what it looks like to "offer your soul" to others—not just scripture or advice.
- Read 1 Thessalonians 2:7–8 and talk about what it means to cherish others like family.

Weekend Reflection:

As a group, brainstorm one tangible way you can "be the message" together—perhaps serving in your community, blessing a neighbor, or helping someone in need. Pray together, asking God to use you to model the gospel with gentleness, grace, and genuine love.

_____

_____

_____

_____

_____

_____

_____

_____

_____

_____

_____

_____

_____

_____

DON'T LET TIME DO A NUMBER ON YOU

To everything there is a season, and a time to every purpose under the heaven.

ECCLESIASTES 3:1 (KJV)

"Time is more than a ticking clock; it's a divine countdown. Use it wisely."

Today is unique—not just because of what's happening in it, but because it's numbered. We mark it on calendars. We count it by hours. We define it with digits. And in a world run by numbers, it's easy to overlook the most important one: the time you have right now.

Maybe you are familiar with The Time Bank Story, which goes like this: Imagine for a moment that your phone buzzes early one morning. You glance at the screen, and it's a message from your bank. The message says, "Congratulations! You've been given a brand-new account. Starting today, $86,400 will be deposited into your account every single morning. But there's a catch—whatever you don't use by midnight disappears. You can't save it, you can't roll it over, and you can't transfer it. You either spend it or lose it."

Now stop and think—what would you do? Would you let that money just slip away? Of course not! You'd use every dollar you could. You'd invest it, you'd try to make it count—or at least I hope that would be your aim.

But here's the twist—this story isn't about money. It's about something far more valuable. You already have that kind of account. Every morning, God credits you with 86,400 seconds.

Just like that bank account, what you don't use wisely is gone forever at midnight. You can't borrow from tomorrow. You can't get a refund from yesterday. You only have what's in front of you today.

And here's the reality: Time doesn't care who you are. The wealthy don't get more of it, and the poor don't get less of it. Every single one of us wakes up with the same deposit. The question is, what will we do with it?

Some people waste it on regret. Some lose it chasing things that don't last. But the wise invest it in people, in purpose, in things that matter.

Because when it's gone, it's gone. Money lost can be made again. Time lost is gone forever.

So don't just count your days—make your days count. When the clock strikes midnight tonight, and today's deposit is gone, let it be said that you spent it well, because it's all about the numbers.

Think about it—when we talk about jobs, we say, "I work a 9 to 5." We fly on 747s. We drive at 65. We call 911 in emergencies and 411 for information. Golfers play 18 holes, and many try their luck playing numbers in hopes of sudden wealth. We celebrate 21 as a milestone and fear turning 70 or 80 as if it means the end. We obsess over credit scores, follower counts, cholesterol levels, and election polls.

We're told to give 100%, and if we're good enough, maybe we'll be number 1. But I'd argue that the most life-altering number of all is 24 —as in, 24 hours in a day. Because no matter your background, bank account, or last name, this is the number God gives equally to all. And what you do with it will either multiply your life or minimize your impact.

John Maxwell said it best: "We over-exaggerate yesterday, overestimate tomorrow, and underestimate today." You can't change yesterday—it's done. You can't count on tomorrow—it's not promised. But today—today you can change everything.

And I would argue that if you change your habits today, you will change your future. Change your attitude today, and you change your relationships. Change your mindset today, and you rewrite your destiny.

I remember learning how to tell time in kindergarten, but it wasn't until later in life that I learned how to use it. And because of that, many of us grow up with warped views of time—treating it as if it can be recycled or redone.

Let me say it plainly: Don't let time do a number on you.

We recycle plastics, bottles, and even fashion—but the one thing you can't recycle is wasted time. Time is that one commodity you can never retrieve once it's gone. You can apologize for how you spent it. You can try to make up for it. But you can't reclaim it.

And yet, people waste it as if it's infinite—as if the clock on the wall is a suggestion and not a statement of reality.

Time-management expert Kevin Kruse interviewed more than 200 ultra-successful people—billionaires, Olympians, and CEOs. Not one of them credited their success to a to-do list.

Why? Because a to-do list doesn't account for the value of time—it just stacks tasks. It's an inventory, not a strategy. Successful people don't just plan what to do—they plan when to do it. They assign time blocks. They calendar their priorities, not just their projects.

They understand something powerful: what's not scheduled is seldom done. Because here's the truth: Time is linear. It doesn't loop. It moves in one direction.

Time is limited. You get 24 hours. That's it. You can lose money and earn it back—but time? Once it's gone, it's gone. And last but not least, time is life. Waste your time, and you waste your life.

And Scripture agrees. Daniel 2:20–21 reminds us that time is not just a number on a watch—it's in the hands of God: "He changes the times and the seasons…" Time shifts under His authority, not ours.

Then there is something to be regarded concerning time and eternity. Psalm 90:10 says, "The days of our lives are seventy years; and if by reason of strength they are eighty… it is soon cut off, and we fly away." This verse doesn't just measure time—it mourns its speed. It reminds us that time is short, life is swift, and eternity is long.

We live like there's no end, but the truth is, time moves quickly, often too quickly. And many people only wake up to the value of time when they've already lost most of it.

Jesus, in Luke 12:56, puts it even more directly: "You can discern the face of the sky and of the earth, but how is it you do not discern this time? " We track stock trends, news alerts, and social media movements, but we miss the signs of God speaking through the clock of our lives.

We get anxious about deadlines but ignore the ultimate one—our accountability before God for how we spent the days He gave us.

Time is not to be marked; it's meant to be used. Don't just count the hours. Make the hours count. Don't just mark time—use time to make your mark.

Ask yourself:

- What am I doing today that echoes in eternity?
- What relationships am I building?
- What seeds am I sowing?
- What legacy am I living into?

Remember, every breath you take is a borrowed moment. Every sunrise is a divine opportunity. And every day you live is a chance to do something eternal with the temporary.

Your calendar may be full. Your week may be scheduled. But God's calling you to live intentionally. So, reclaim the power of now. Honor the purpose in this season. Step out of delay and into divine urgency. Redeem the time, for the days are evil (Ephesians 5:16).

God doesn't just want you to manage time—He wants you to master it. Steward it like the treasure it is. Use it like it's kingdom currency. Spend it on what matters, not on what distracts.

Don't let time do a number on you. You've got 24 today. Let it reflect something eternal.

Do something today that time can't erase. Because time is ticking —but purpose is calling.

LIVING THE LESSON

Throughout the week, take time to put into practice what you've read and reflected on. Each daily activity offers an opportunity to deepen your faith and live out the lessons from this devotional. On the following pages, engage with these activities to grow spiritually and strengthen your relationship with God and others.

Monday | Scripture Focus & Reflection

Start the week reflecting on how you view and value time in your daily life.

- Ecclesiastes 3:1
- Psalm 90:12
- Daniel 2:20–21

Reflection Questions:

- How have you been using your time lately: wisely or wastefully?
- Are there areas in your life where you're "marking time" but not making a mark?
- What spiritual significance do you see in the time and season you're currently in?

Journaling Prompt:

Write about how your relationship with time has shaped your growth —spiritually, personally, or professionally. How can you begin redeeming the time God has given you starting today?

_____
_____
_____
_____
_____
_____
_____
_____
_____
_____
_____

Tuesday | Personal Prayer & Petition

Dedicate time today to pray for discipline, focus, and a divine sense of urgency in fulfilling your purpose.

Prayer Focus:

- Ask God to help you see time as a gift and use it with intentionality.
- Repent for wasted moments and ask for wisdom to prioritize what matters most.
- Petition for clarity about the season you're in and the assignments connected to it.

Journaling Prompt:

What is one major area where you need God's help to manage your time better? What would "fruitfulness" look like in that area? Write a prayer of surrender, asking God to help you steward your time for His glory.

_____

_____

_____

_____

_____

_____

_____

_____

_____

_____

_____

_____

_____

_____

Wednesday | Midweek Worship & Gratitude

Worship God for the gift of time, and His faithfulness through every season.

Worship Song Suggestions:

- "Seasons" – Hillsong Worship
- "My Times Are in Your Hands" – Marty Nystrom
- "Alpha and Omega" – Israel & New Breed

Gratitude List:

- List 3 moments in your life when God made divine use of time (a delay, a perfect open door, or a timely blessing).
- Thank God for the current season you're in, even if it's challenging.
- Praise Him for being a God who doesn't waste time, and who teaches us how to redeem ours.

_____
_____
_____
_____
_____
_____
_____
_____
_____
_____
_____
_____
_____
_____

Thursday | Outreach & Encouragement

Encourage someone today to make the most of the time and season they're in. Speak life and urgency over their purpose.

Outreach Ideas:

- Call, text, or email a friend who seems stuck or discouraged. Remind them: *"This is still your time."*
- Share Ecclesiastes 3:1 with someone who's in transition and doesn't yet see the purpose in their season.
- Post a social media reminder: *"Don't just mark time; make your mark. This day matters."*

Journaling Prompt:

How did encouraging someone else about their time and purpose challenge you to reflect on your own? What did it stir in you?

_____
_____
_____
_____
_____
_____
_____
_____
_____
_____
_____
_____
_____
_____
_____
_____
_____

Friday | Self-Examination & Recommitment

Take a serious look at how you've spent your time this week. Where can you improve?

Reflection Questions:

- Did I honor God with how I used my time this week?
- Were there moments of distraction, procrastination, or avoidance?
- What habits or patterns need to shift to help me steward time more wisely?

Journaling Prompt:

Write a declaration of recommitment to using your time for God's purposes. Be specific: How will you adjust your habits, your calendar, or your mindset moving forward?

_____
_____
_____
_____
_____
_____
_____
_____
_____
_____
_____
_____
_____
_____
_____

Saturday & Sunday | Family Activity & Reflection

This weekend, have a family or group conversation about time, priorities, and purpose.

Group Discussion Ideas:

- What does it mean to "redeem the time" as a family or community?
- How can we spend more intentional time with God *and* with each other?
- What's one way we can make this season meaningful together?

Weekend Reflection:

Create a family or group "time audit." Identify what activities consume the most time, and whether those things are life-giving or time-draining. Close in prayer, asking God to help you become better stewards of your time, together.

_____

_____

_____

_____

_____

_____

_____

_____

_____

_____

_____

_____

_____

_____

DON'T OVERLOOK THE OBVIOUS

And he turned to the woman, and said unto Simon,
Seest thou this woman? I entered into thine house, thou
gavest me no water for my feet: but she hath washed my
feet with tears, and wiped them with the hairs of her
head.

LUKE 7:44 (KJV)

"Don't overlook the obvious."

A psychology professor once shared an experience that left him both humbled and amused. Rushing across campus, burdened with books and worried about being late, he wanted to check the time. His phone was buried in his backpack, and though he wore a watch, his hands were too full to check it.

If I were preaching this, I'd pause and say, "This might be your biggest problem—you're carrying too many burdens to realize what time it is! " But of course, I'll save that for another day. (smile)

Suddenly, the bell tower on campus chimed. He looked up to acknowledge it, and, for the first time—after 21 years of teaching there—he noticed the clock face staring back at him. He had been working under that clock all those years and never realized the time was always visible—right above him.

In other words, he had overlooked the obvious. And my question to you is, how often do we do the same? We search for direction when the sign is already lit. We question God's presence when His finger-prints are all over our lives. We beg for confirmation, ignoring the very evidence that's been shouting in plain view.

We look everywhere for answers that have already been revealed. We chase affirmation that God already provides. And we miss the blessings right in front of us because we're too distracted by what's behind or burdened by what we're carrying.

And although we live in a time when information is endless, many times revelation can still be ignored. For all our knowledge, we still overlook the obvious. How often have we taken waking up for granted? Or assumed good health, peace, or provision were owed to us? How many times has God moved in our favor, but we failed to say thank you?

Sometimes we are so burdened, so busy, or so self-sufficient that we fail to look up and see what God is doing right in front of us.

In our Spiritual Vitamin, Jesus turns to Simon the Pharisee and says, "Do you see this woman? " It's not that Simon was blind, it's just that he couldn't see. He had missed what was obvious. As a matter of fact, humanity has demonstrated a tendency to miss the obvious, even when it's staring us in the face.

Glaciers are melting, storms are intensifying, and coastlines are shrinking—all observable, all measurable. And yet, many continue to argue as if nothing is happening. The evidence is as plain as the rising sea levels, but denial blinds us.

We choke on the very air we breathe; rivers turn toxic, plastic floats in every ocean while companies swim in profit, and consumers look away. We walk past it daily but fail to see the slow erosion of our health and habitat.

There is enough food in the world to feed every person, yet millions starve while tons of food are wasted. The abundance and the lack exist side by side—but somehow, we normalize the contradiction.

Preventable diseases still kill millions, even when cures exist. Vaccines, sanitation, clean water—simple answers within arm's reach —yet ignored or inaccessible. The obvious solution is right there, but humanity continues to stumble in blindness.

The real danger isn't simply the crisis itself, but our blindness to it. When the obvious becomes invisible, when truth is ignored, we condemn ourselves to destruction. In philosophy, this is the "crisis of perception"—the inability to acknowledge reality, even when reality is undeniable.

The paradox of human perception is this: we often overlook what is most obvious, most urgent, and most vital. Like a fish unaware of the water it swims in, we can be surrounded by reality and yet blind to it.

This is why prophets, reformers, and visionaries have always been dismissed—because they point to what everyone should see, but most refuse to see.

While Simon sat in smug silence, a woman—broken, forgiven, grateful—washed Jesus' feet with her tears and wiped them with her hair. She anointed Him with love. Simon, on the other hand, gave no water, no kiss, no oil—no honor.

She recognized her sin and her salvation. He assumed he had neither. She saw grace. He saw only her past. Jesus wasn't rebuking Simon because the woman was better. He was trying to help him see what should have been obvious. He was showing him that forgiveness recognized is worship released.

Why, you might ask, am I making such a big deal about this? Simply because, too often, we treat the presence of Jesus as casual—familiar, and sometimes even take it for granted.

Simon sees the scene unfold, but he misses what is obvious. He sees the woman, but not her worship. He sees her past, but not her repentance. He sees Jesus sitting at his table, but not the Savior sitting in his presence. Simon missed the opportunity to worship because he thought he didn't need it.

Simon had the Son of God reclining in his home, yet he treated Him as ordinary. No water for His feet. No kiss of greeting. No oil of honor. Why? Because Simon, like so many of us, missed the obvious.

And isn't that what we still do today? We can quote His words but miss His worth. We can attend His house but overlook His presence. We can sit in the same room with Jesus and never recognize who He truly is.

It's the tragedy of the obvious. We can see the forest but miss the fire consuming it. We track the stars in galaxies millions of light-years away but cannot notice the trash in our own streets. The tragedy of our age has not become ignorance itself, but rather the refusal to recognize what is obvious.

The Messiah came, not hidden in shadows, but walking openly in their streets, healing their sick, and raising their dead. Luke 7:14 tells us, "Young man, I say to thee, arise." And the dead sat up! Yet people still doubted, still debated, and still dismissed Him.

And I would contend that Simon's problem is still our problem: we take the presence of Jesus for granted. We normalize what should astonish us. We reduce what should overwhelm us. We miss the obvious, because seeing Him for who He is demands more than casual religion—it demands surrender.

But the woman? She didn't overlook the obvious. She knew:

- Who Jesus was
- What He'd done
- And how undeserving she was

And as a result, her gratitude exploded in action.

How grateful are you for the presence of Jesus in your life? It will show in your worship. Psalm 51:17 reminds us, "The sacrifices of God are a broken spirit, a broken and contrite heart—these, O God, You will not despise."

Sometimes, we just need a spiritual reboot. You know the drill—your device freezes, nothing's responding, and the only solution is to shut it down and start over.

And usually, before the reboot, a good technician will always advise, "Save what matters, or it may be lost."

Today, with this Spiritual Vitamin in mind, I pray you'll reboot your priorities:

- Start paying more attention to the obvious.
- Put more wonder into your witness.
- Prioritize your worship.

Don't let the moment pass without recognizing the blessing in it. We often get stuck staring at locked doors and miss the ones that are wide open. We let familiarity rob us of awe. But when we stay present, tuned in, and expectant—what's obvious becomes sacred.

God is often closer than we think. Answers are more visible than we realize. And blessings are more present than we give them credit for. But here is the revelatory takeaway: the obvious is often ignored because it demands change, and change is uncomfortable. Humanity would rather debate the evidence than deal with the consequences.

And so, as a parting thought, I leave you with four areas where I believe we frequently miss the obvious:

1. **Relationships:** We seek extraordinary connections while ignoring the faithful people already showing up daily. Honor the ones who stay.
2. **Provision:** We crave more while forgetting how far God has brought us. If He did it before, He can do it again.
3. **Calling:** We wait for a neon sign when God already placed purpose in our hands—right where we are.
4. **Time:** We procrastinate because we think we have more time. But the clock is always ticking.

Elisha prayed for his servant's eyes to be opened—and suddenly, he saw what had always been there: a heavenly army surrounding them. What if you're surrounded by blessings right now but can't see them because your focus is off?

Today, I invite you to pause. Take inventory. And give thanks—not just for what you hope will come, but for what's already here.

Don't overlook the obvious. Let your praise reflect your awareness. Let your worship reflect your gratitude. And let your life reflect the truth: that God has been here all along—working, blessing, and speaking… right in front of your eyes.

LIVING THE LESSON

Throughout the week, take time to put into practice what you've read and reflected on. Each daily activity offers an opportunity to deepen your faith and live out the lessons from this devotional. On the following pages, engage with these activities to grow spiritually and strengthen your relationship with God and others.

Monday | Scripture Focus & Reflection

Begin your week by reflecting on the overlooked blessings and spiritual truths that are right in front of you.

- Luke 7:44
- Psalm 51:17
- Romans 5:8

Reflection Questions:

- What "obvious" blessings have you recently taken for granted?
- How does your awareness of God's forgiveness shape your daily life?
- Are there signs, moments, or people you've been overlooking that point you back to God?

Journaling Prompt:

Write about something God has done recently that you didn't recognize as significant until now. How is He inviting you to pause, acknowledge, and respond in gratitude today?

_____
_____
_____
_____
_____
_____
_____
_____
_____
_____
_____

Tuesday | Personal Prayer & Petition

Spend time in prayer asking God to help you recognize His presence in the ordinary and be sensitive to His movement in your life.

Prayer Focus:

- Ask God to open your eyes to the everyday signs of His love, correction, and grace.
- Thank Him for the "obvious" blessings—salvation, daily breath, relationships, purpose.
- Petition for renewed spiritual sensitivity to what He's already placed in your life.

Journaling Prompt:

What is God trying to show you right now that you may be overlooking? Write a prayer of humility and surrender, asking Him to help you see with fresh eyes.

_____
_____
_____
_____
_____
_____
_____
_____
_____
_____
_____
_____
_____
_____
_____

Wednesday | Midweek Worship & Gratitude

Worship God for the daily blessings you often overlook—His forgiveness, His nearness, and His grace.

Worship Song Suggestions:

- "Goodness of God" – CeCe Winans
- "Great Are You Lord" – All Sons & Daughters
- "Never Would Have Made It" – Marvin Sapp

Gratitude List:

- List five everyday blessings you tend to take for granted (e.g., breath, peace of mind, the ability to worship freely).
- Thank God for the gift of forgiveness and the privilege of being in relationship with Him.
- Worship Him with a heart of awareness, acknowledging His consistent presence.

_____
_____
_____
_____
_____
_____
_____
_____
_____
_____
_____
_____
_____
_____
_____
_____

Thursday | Outreach & Encouragement

Encourage someone today to pause and reflect on the blessings in their life. Help them not to overlook the obvious.

Outreach Ideas:

- Share Luke 7:44 with someone and ask: "What are you grateful for today?"
- Send a voice message, text, or note to a friend reminding them how far they've come with God's help.
- Encourage someone who feels stuck by helping them identify areas where God *is* working—even if it's subtle.

Journaling Prompt:

How did sharing with others help you see your own life differently? Reflect on how God uses community to highlight the things we sometimes miss.

_____
_____
_____
_____
_____
_____
_____
_____
_____
_____
_____
_____
_____
_____

Friday | Self-Examination & Recommitment

Examine how you've approached your week. Have you honored or overlooked the obvious?

Reflection Questions:

- Have I treated God's presence, provision, or people in my life casually?
- What have I failed to express gratitude for?
- Is there any spiritual "baggage" I need to release in order to see clearly?

Journaling Prompt:

Write a prayer of recommitment, asking God to make you more mindful. Ask Him to help you notice and respond to the obvious signs of His love, direction, and grace in your daily life.

_____

_____

_____

_____

_____

_____

_____

_____

_____

_____

_____

_____

_____

_____

_____

_____

_____

Saturday & Sunday | Family Activity & Reflection

This weekend, gather your family or loved ones to reflect on the theme "Don't overlook the obvious."

Group Discussion Ideas:

- Share moments when you recognized God's hand in a situation—only in hindsight.
- Read Luke 7:36–50 together and talk about the difference between Simon and the woman.
- Reflect on how gratitude leads to deeper love and awareness of God's presence.

Weekend Reflection:

Take time together to list 10 things each person is thankful for, especially "ordinary" things. Then pray as a group, thanking God for the obvious and not-so-obvious ways He blesses, forgives, and leads. Choose one shared action you can take this week to live with more gratitude and awareness.

_____
_____
_____
_____
_____
_____
_____
_____
_____
_____
_____
_____
_____

FOR GRANTED

When I said, My foot slippeth; thy mercy, O Lord, held me up.

PSALM 94:18 (KJV)

"Don't take mercy for granted."

We live in an age that's made us numb to wonder. A culture of convenience has dulled our appreciation for life's most valuable gifts. We scroll past beauty, skim past blessings, and sleepwalk through opportunities. We even take our freedom for granted, our natural world for granted. Our breath, our blessings, and even our burdens—many of which are lighter than they could be—we treat with casual disregard.

But most sobering of all is this: we often take God's mercy for granted. Why, you might ask? Because mercy is quiet. It's not always visible or loud. It doesn't demand attention—but it holds us together.

It works behind the scenes, under the radar, in the margins of our failures and the fractures of our soul.

Mercy shows up when we slip. The psalmist confesses, "When I said, My foot slippeth; thy mercy, O Lord, held me up." Mercy met him mid-slip.

If I could pause right here, I would have you take note that in the verse quoted from the psalmist, "foot" is symbolic of our walk—our journey, our life-path. "Slippeth" speaks to drifting, veering off course, getting distracted, disoriented, or becoming disobedient. This is not a violent fall. It's subtle. It's the unsteady moment when the ground beneath you gives way and you realize just how little control you really have.

Ever been there? Of course. We all have. And in those moments—moments of weakness, misdirection, and missed priorities—mercy steps in. Quietly. Faithfully. Powerfully. And here is what I have come to appreciate:

- Mercy doesn't shame. It steadies.
- Mercy doesn't condemn. It catches.
- Mercy doesn't accuse. It upholds.

We often think mercy is for the big failures—the rock-bottom moments. But the truth is, it's for the everyday stumbles too. Mercy is the reason your worst day didn't end you. Mercy is the reason you're still here, still breathing, still capable of getting it right the next time.

And most importantly, mercy is the evidence of God's love. The writer reminds us in Lamentations that "it is the Lord's mercy that we are not consumed," and that "His compassions fail not."

We sometimes only learn to value mercy through our failings. Think of Peter—the disciple who boldly proclaimed loyalty but later denied Christ. He knew failure. But more importantly, he came to know mercy.

After the denial came restoration. After the stumble came support. Why? Because mercy is God's lovingkindness in action. It's the divine reset that reminds us God is not keeping score to reject but keeping grace to restore.

- Mercy is what keeps you from getting what you deserve.
- Mercy is what allows grace to have the final say.
- Mercy is what saves you when justice is ready to strike.

As I previously mentioned, Lamentations 3:22–23 reminds us, "It is of the Lord's mercies that we are not consumed," but I failed to add, "They are new every morning." What does that mean? Simply this: it is not yesterday's mercy keeping you afloat today—it's a fresh batch, made just for this moment. Like cookies in the oven. (Sorry, that just came to mind.)

Somebody ought to thank God for the mercy that is not only like a fresh batch of cookies from the oven but also covers like fresh snow—beautifying what it touches, softening what it surrounds.

Mercy isn't just a feeling; it's a force. Mercy is not soft. It's not passive. It's not weak. It's the divine will of God intervening in the human mess. To take God's mercy for granted is to live as if His patience will last forever, as if His grace is a license, as if His longsuffering is weakness. Mercy is meant to move us to repentance, not give us room for rebellion.

- It's the grip that steadies when your footing gives out.
- It's the lifeline that catches you mid-fall.
- It's the shield that blocks the worst of what could've been.

Every day we wake up with breath in our lungs, though we didn't earn it, consider it an expression of God's mercies. We drive past accidents that could have been ours—God's mercies. We recover from mistakes that could have destroyed us—mercy. And know this: when the weight of life tries to pull you under, mercy is what will hold you up. These are all expressions of God's mercies—but how often do we shrug and go on as if it's nothing?

Societies endure despite corruption, injustice, and moral collapse, not because they deserve survival, but because God is still holding back judgment. Yet history shows us: mercy delayed is not mercy denied.

The fact that God gives us "another chance" is not because He overlooks sin, but because He desires repentance. But when we treat His mercy like an endless resource, we abuse it rather than appreciate it.

David, who penned Psalm 94, knew something about slips. He had missteps with power, with people, and with personal discipline. And yet, God didn't discard him. Why? Mercy. And that mercy made David a man after God's own heart—not because he was perfect, but because he repented, remembered, and revered God's mercy.

My dear brothers and sisters, don't let familiarity breed contempt when it comes to God's mercies. The more we receive mercy, the easier it is to forget we didn't earn it.

- That job you still have after mistakes? Mercy.
- That relationship that survived your rough season? Mercy.
- That healing you weren't sure you'd experience? Mercy.
- That second (or third, or fourth) chance? Mercy.

And sometimes, it's the mercy we don't even notice—the traps we never saw, the breakdowns that didn't happen, and the tears we didn't cry. The accident that didn't occur. The diagnosis that never came. The temptation we were spared from. All are equally expressions of God's mercies.

Make no mistake about it, all of it is a result of mercy. So let us not become so accustomed to being covered that we forget to be grateful. Gratitude, after all, is the memory of the heart. It keeps us from spiritual amnesia and emotional entitlement.

I remember once stepping out of my car during a snowstorm, not realizing the driveway had iced over. My foot hit the ground, and I instantly slipped—nothing to grab, nothing to brace myself with. Just down I went. No traction. No warning. No support.

It taught me something that I will never forget: when you fall and there's nothing to hold you up, you hit hard. But thank God, spiritually, that's no longer the case...because of the One "who is able to keep us from falling"...that's not our story.

God's mercy is that invisible hand beneath us. That grace cushion, if you will, that breaks our fall and braces us until we find our footing again. We may slip—but we don't have to fall fatally. And even when we fall, we don't hit rock bottom.

Psalm 94 says, "When I said, 'My foot is slipping,' your unfailing love, Lord, supported me." That's mercy. Again, mercy is God pulling us up when we should have gone under. Mercy is God's hand rescuing us when the ice of sin should have taken us down.

But here's the danger: what if we start treating mercy like a game? What if, instead of crying out, "Lord, my foot is slipping," we keep saying, "I'll be fine"? That's, my friend, when mercy turns into presumption. That's when we take for granted the very hand that's holding us.

The Good News is God's mercy is real. His compassions are new every morning. But mercy was never meant to be tested—it was meant to be treasured. Because the truth is, every step we take could have been the one that broke us, but His mercy supported us.

The warning before us is clear: don't take mercy for granted. Every sunrise, every second chance, every time He pulls us back from the edge—that's not entitlement, that's mercy. And the question is, how long will we keep walking on thin ice before we fall to our knees in gratitude?

- Don't take mercy for granted.
- Don't let spiritual entitlement rob you of gratitude.
- Don't allow success to blind you to the Source.
- Don't treat daily mercies like background noise.

Because at the end of the day, the truth is, what's holding you up might be the very thing you've stopped thanking God for. You didn't keep yourself together. Mercy did. You didn't recover all by yourself.

Mercy helped. You didn't escape because you were wise. Mercy stepped in.

Mercy is holding you—don't ignore it. Don't overlook it, and by all means, don't take it for granted.

LIVING THE LESSON

Throughout the week, take time to put into practice what you've read and reflected on. Each daily activity offers an opportunity to deepen your faith and live out the lessons from this devotional. On the following pages, engage with these activities to grow spiritually and strengthen your relationship with God and others.

Monday | Scripture Focus & Reflection

Start the week with a deep reflection on the mercy of God that has carried and covered you.

- Psalm 94:18
- Lamentations 3:22–23
- Titus 3:5

Reflection Questions:

- When was the last time you paused to thank God specifically for His mercy?
- In what area of your life have you slipped, yet God's mercy held you up?
- How has God's mercy protected you from consequences you deserved?

Journaling Prompt:

Write about a time when you knew God's mercy carried you. Reflect on how different things could have been without His intervention. Thank Him for being the One who holds you when you slip.

_____
_____
_____
_____
_____
_____
_____
_____
_____
_____
_____
_____

Tuesday | Personal Prayer & Petition

Set aside time today to pray for a fresh awareness and appreciation of God's mercy in your life.

Prayer Focus:

- Thank God for the countless times His mercy covered you, especially in unseen ways.
- Ask Him to reveal any areas where you've been taking His grace for granted.
- Petition for a humble and repentant heart that honors His kindness.

Journaling Prompt:

What does God's mercy mean to you, personally? Are there areas of your life where you need to stop treating His grace casually? Write out a heartfelt prayer of gratitude and renewed reverence.

_____

_____

_____

_____

_____

_____

_____

_____

_____

_____

_____

_____

_____

_____

Wednesday | Midweek Worship & Gratitude

Let your worship today flow from a place of pure thanksgiving for mercy that holds you up when you slip.

Worship Song Suggestions:

- "Mercy" – Elevation Worship
- "Your Mercy" – Paul Baloche
- "Great Is Thy Faithfulness" – CeCe Winans (Morning by Morning)

Gratitude List:

- List three specific "slips" (moments of failure or weakness) that didn't end in disaster because God's mercy stepped in.
- Write a thank-you letter to God, celebrating the mercy that keeps showing up for you, day after day.

_____

_____

_____

_____

_____

_____

_____

_____

_____

_____

_____

_____

_____

_____

_____

Thursday | Outreach & Encouragement

Encourage someone who may be burdened by guilt, failure, or shame. Remind them: *Mercy is still available.*

Outreach Ideas:

- Share Psalm 94:18 with someone who feels like they've failed or fallen.
- Write a text or note that says: *"God's mercy doesn't run out. It's holding you up, even now."*
- Offer to pray with a friend who's wrestling with discouragement or shame.

Journaling Prompt:

How did sharing God's mercy with someone else affect your view of it? Reflect on how being a messenger of mercy brings healing, both to others and to yourself.

_____

_____

_____

_____

_____

_____

_____

_____

_____

_____

_____

_____

_____

_____

_____

Friday | Self-Examination & Recommitment

Today, take time to examine where you've taken God's mercy for granted, and recommit to walking in humility and awareness.

Reflection Questions:

- Have I treated God's mercy like a safety net instead of a sacred gift?
- What patterns, relationships, or habits have I tolerated because I assumed "God will cover me"?
- How can I walk in deeper reverence for the mercy that has kept me?

Journaling Prompt:

Write down one area of your life where you've been careless with grace. What would it look like to live with more intentionality and honor toward God's mercy in that area? Recommit your heart to walking wisely and humbly.

_____
_____
_____
_____
_____
_____
_____
_____
_____
_____
_____
_____
_____
_____

Saturday & Sunday | Family Activity & Reflection

Use this weekend to reflect together on the mercy of God. Share stories and discuss how mercy has shaped your family's journey.

Group Discussion Ideas:

- Share testimonies of when you or a family member "slipped," but God's mercy held you up.
- Read Psalm 94:18 aloud and discuss what it means for each person.
- Talk about how to be more merciful toward one another, modeling God's grace in your home.

Weekend Reflection:

Create a "Mercy Memory List" as a family—documenting times God stepped in with mercy. Pray together, thanking God for His sustaining grace and asking Him to help you never take His mercy—or each other—for granted.

_____

_____

_____

_____

_____

_____

_____

_____

_____

_____

_____

_____

_____

_____

THE POSSIBILITY

And Jesus said unto them, Because of your unbelief: for verily I say unto you, If ye have faith as a grain of mustard seed, ye shall say unto this mountain, Remove hence to yonder place; and it shall remove; and nothing shall be impossible unto you.

MATTHEW 17:20 (KJV)

"Embrace the possibility."

———

One of the biggest success stories in this era of social media and technological advancement is the story of Mark Zuckerberg. A college dropout turned tech pioneer, Zuckerberg founded one of the largest social media platforms the world has ever seen—Facebook. His vision revolutionized global communication and forever altered the way people connect, share, and build communities online.

But Zuckerberg's success wasn't born of privilege or perfection—it was born of possibility. He believed that people wanted to share more about their lives online, and he acted on that belief. He didn't just dream it. He did it. And not only did he benefit, but those who partnered with him—who believed with him—benefited as well. Here is the principle: possibilities don't just lift individuals; they elevate communities.

That's the lesson for us all: only those who see the invisible will accomplish the impossible.

Jesus made the same point long before Zuckerberg launched his idea from a Harvard dorm room. In our Spiritual Vitamin, Jesus teaches His disciples that if they had faith the size of a mustard seed, they could speak to a mountain and command it to move—and it would. Nothing would be impossible to them. Nothing.

Now, we must understand that the phrase "removing mountains" was a common Jewish metaphor used to describe overcoming large and difficult obstacles. And let's be honest, life is full of them. Mountains of disappointment. Mountains of debt. Mountains of grief. Mountains of sickness. Mountains of doubt. We all face them. But Jesus wasn't emphasizing the mountain. He was emphasizing the faith.

Faith doesn't need to be massive. It just needs to be present, real, and rooted. Let that sink in.

The size of the mountain isn't the issue—it's the size of your belief.

You don't need a truckload of faith to change your situation. Just a seed will do. A mustard seed. Small, yet packed with promise. Fragile-looking, yet filled with force. Because faith, no matter how small, has power when it's placed in the right source.

Faith isn't about flexing; it's about focusing. Not about performance, but persistence. Not about shouting louder, but believing deeper.

Faith redefines limitations. It reshapes expectations. And it reframes what we think is possible. Where fear sees a wall, faith sees a window. Where logic says, "It's over," faith whispers, "It's just beginning."

Where man says, "Can't be done," faith says, "Watch God do it."

Matthew 17:20 wasn't just a lesson in belief—it was a correction for unbelief. The disciples couldn't cast out a demon from a suffering boy, and they asked Jesus why. His answer? "Because of your unbelief." He didn't say it was because they lacked training, talent, or titles. It was belief they lacked—possibility thinking rooted in kingdom authority.

We still wrestle with the same problem today.

We believe God can… we're just not sure He will—for us.

We think miracles are reserved for missionaries, or pastors, or those with spotless records. We don't feel qualified for the impossible. But faith doesn't require credentials. It just requires conviction.

Charles Spurgeon put it this way:

"If thy faith be of the mustard-seed kind… if thou canst only say, 'Lord, I believe, help thou mine unbelief,'… then Christ will be the end of the law for righteousness to thee."

Faith is the power to embrace the possibilities of God. Jesus said that with just a mustard seed of faith, mountains can move. Think about that—the mountain represents the immovable, the impossible, the obstacle that stands in your way. Unbelief will sit at the bottom of that mountain and complain. Faith will speak to the mountain and command it to move.

Faith isn't blind optimism—it's radical trust. It's looking at the impossible and saying, "I believe God can." Abraham embraced the possibility of a child in old age. Peter embraced the possibility of walking on water. Mary embraced the possibility of birthing the Savior of the world. And every one of them saw God do the impossible.

So here's the challenge: we must never allow ourselves to settle for unbelief. Don't stop at what your eyes see. Embrace the possibilities of what God can do when faith, even the size of a mustard seed, is planted in Him. You don't need perfect faith—you need present faith. So, let me ask you today:

- What mountain are you facing?
- What diagnosis has shaken your hope?

- What financial burden is making you question your future?
- What dream have you buried because you thought it was too late?

Jesus didn't say, "Maybe it will move." He said it shall. Not because of magic, but because of trust. Because of belief. Because of the unshakable power of possibility.

"Nothing shall be impossible unto you." That's not a motivational slogan—it's a divine promise.

And let me add this: sometimes the mountain doesn't move all at once. Sometimes it moves pebble by pebble, step by step. Sometimes God doesn't remove the mountain—He gives you the strength to climb it. Either way, faith makes it possible.

And don't be surprised when God calls you to speak to the mountain. Notice, Jesus said, "You shall say…" That means your voice has power when it's filled with faith. Your declaration is the beginning of your deliverance.

Speak it: "This debt will not define me."
Speak it: "This sickness will not silence me."
Speak it: "This setback will not stop me."
Speak it: "This mountain will move."

There is something powerful about giving voice to your vision, about putting faith on your lips.

God specializes in impossible things. He opened a sea. He brought down walls. He raised the dead. He restored broken people and redeemed lost causes. That's not fairy-tale faith—that's mountain-moving faith.

And the same God who did it then is still doing it now. So, here's the call: embrace the possibility.

Even if your faith trembles. Even if it's mixed with questions. Even if you don't have it all figured out—believe. Because if you have faith the size of a mustard seed, you have more than enough.

More than enough to *try* again.
More than enough to *hope* again.
More than enough to *pray* again.
More than enough to *speak* again.
More than enough to *see* the impossible become possible.

Abraham (Romans 4:20–21): He staggered not at the promise of God through unbelief, but was strong in faith, being fully persuaded that what God had promised, He was able also to perform. Abraham embraced possibilities others would laugh at.

Peter (Matthew 14:29): When Peter stepped out of the boat, he embraced the possibility of walking on water. Unbelief would have kept him seated, but faith allowed him to step.

Mary (Luke 1:38): A virgin, told she would bear the Son of God—impossible to human reasoning. Yet she said, "Be it unto me according to thy word." She embraced divine possibilities.

Don't let doubt dictate your destiny.
Don't let fear frame your future.
Don't let the mountain convince you that your faith doesn't matter.

Speak to it, trust through it, and believe beyond it. Which brings me to my final point of emphasis: note Jesus says, "nothing shall be impossible unto you." The Greek transliterated emphasis is not just that obstacles might move, but that there is no situation in which you will be without divine power if you walk in faith.

The phrase points not merely to "possibility" but to empowerment —God supplying strength where human strength is absent or insufficient. When Jesus said, "Nothing shall be impossible unto you," He used the word "adynēsei," meaning "without power." In other words, faith makes sure you are never without power. Faith doesn't eliminate the mountain, but it guarantees you won't face it powerless. Faith plugs you into the dunamis—the explosive power of God—so that what looked immovable must bow to His authority.

And if Jesus said it, you can believe it. Now... embrace the possibility—and watch mountains move.

LIVING THE LESSON

Throughout the week, take time to put into practice what you've read and reflected on. Each daily activity offers an opportunity to deepen your faith and live out the lessons from this devotional. On the following pages, engage with these activities to grow spiritually and strengthen your relationship with God and others.

Monday | Scripture Focus & Reflection

Start the week by meditating on the power of small but genuine faith to move mountains and unlock divine possibilities.

- Matthew 17:20
- Mark 9:23
- Hebrews 11:1

Reflection Questions:

- What "mountain" in your life feels immovable right now?
- Have you dismissed your ability to overcome simply because your faith feels small?
- What would change in your life if you truly believed *nothing is impossible* with God?

Journaling Prompt:

Write about a time when faith—even small and trembling—produced a breakthrough in your life. Reflect on how God's power was magnified through your trust. What possibility do you need to believe for today?

_____

_____

_____

_____

_____

_____

_____

_____

_____

_____

_____

Tuesday | Personal Prayer & Petition

Set time aside today to ask God to revive your belief in what's still possible, even when it feels out of reach.

Prayer Focus:

- Thank God for the measure of faith you already possess.
- Ask Him to help you overcome doubt, fear, or unbelief.
- Petition for strength to hold onto hope, even when the odds feel stacked against you.

Journaling Prompt:

What situation in your life have you given up on too soon? Write a bold faith-filled prayer declaring what you are believing God to do, even if it seems impossible right now.

_____

_____

_____

_____

_____

_____

_____

_____

_____

_____

_____

_____

_____

_____

_____

_____

Wednesday | Midweek Worship & Gratitude

Let your worship rise today from a place of gratitude for the miracles that have already happened—and the ones still unfolding.

Worship Song Suggestions:

- "Do It Again" – Elevation Worship
- "Way Maker" – Leeland
- "Impossible" – Travis Greene

Gratitude List:

- List three things God has done in your life that once felt impossible.
- Write a thank-you letter to God for the unseen ways He's working behind the scenes in your life.

_____
_____
_____
_____
_____
_____
_____
_____
_____
_____
_____
_____
_____
_____
_____
_____
_____
_____

Thursday | Outreach & Encouragement

Today, become a vessel of possibility for someone else who needs to be reminded of what faith can do.

Outreach Ideas:

- Text or call someone going through a hard time and remind them: "Nothing is impossible with God."
- Share Matthew 17:20 with a friend who feels stuck or discouraged.
- Offer to pray with someone who is doubting their next step.

Journaling Prompt:

How did encouraging someone else today impact your own faith? Write about how your words became a reflection of what *you* also needed to hear.

_____
_____
_____
_____
_____
_____
_____
_____
_____
_____
_____
_____
_____
_____
_____

Friday | Self-Examination & Recommitment

Take time to examine areas of unbelief, doubt, or passivity that have kept you from fully embracing possibility.

Reflection Questions:

- Where have I let doubt silence my faith?
- Are there dreams, visions, or prayers I've abandoned because they felt impossible?
- What would it look like to live with mustard-seed faith every day?

Journaling Prompt:

Write down one faith goal you've been afraid to pursue. Recommit it to God and declare your trust that He can make a way, even when you can't see how.

_____
_____
_____
_____
_____
_____
_____
_____
_____
_____
_____
_____
_____
_____
_____
_____

Saturday & Sunday | Family Activity & Reflection

Gather with your family to reflect on faith and the power of believing in what seems impossible.

Group Discussion Ideas:

- Share a story of a time when something impossible happened in your life.
- Read Matthew 17:20 together and talk about what "mountain-moving faith" means.
- Create a "Faith Wall" where each person writes one thing they're believing God for.

Weekend Reflection:

As a family, pray over every "mountain" you listed on your Faith Wall. Ask God to strengthen your belief and open your eyes to see what is possible when you trust Him.

_____
_____
_____
_____
_____
_____
_____
_____
_____
_____
_____
_____
_____
_____
_____
_____

NEWS WILL GET OUT

For there is one God, and one mediator between God
and men, the man Christ Jesus; Who gave himself a
ransom for all, to be testified in due time.

1 TIMOTHY 2:5–6 (KJV)

"Eventually, the news is going to get out."

An unprecedented global cyberattack recently stunned the
world. This particular form of attack, known as
ransomware, locked users out of their systems and
demanded payment to restore access. Appropriately named WannaCry,
the virus didn't just infect individual computers; it targeted networks
across hospitals, banks, universities, and entire government infra-
structures. Its damage was both crippling and sobering.

The term "ransom," in this context, refers to the price demanded
to release something held hostage. But long before technology coined
this term for criminal purposes, Scripture had already embedded it in

our theological vocabulary. Biblically, a ransom is a redemptive price paid to secure the release of someone in bondage. In other words, it is a costly act of mercy.

The Old Testament references ransoms often. In Exodus 30:12, the Lord commands that each Israelite give a ransom for his soul during the census to avoid a plague. And in Hosea 13:14, God promises, "I will ransom them from the power of the grave; I will redeem them from death..." That's the language of love, and I would contend that it is the language of deliverance.

And in our Spiritual Vitamin, the Apostle Paul picks up this redemptive thread and ties it tightly around the person and work of Jesus Christ. He reminds the church that there is only one God and only one Mediator between God and humanity—Jesus, the Christ, who gave Himself as a ransom for all. Here's the shout: You were the one held hostage by sin, and Jesus was the One who paid the price.

Unlike the ransomware that uses coercion to exploit, Jesus offered Himself willingly. His sacrifice wasn't extortion—it was redemption. His death on the cross was the ultimate transaction, satisfying divine justice and securing eternal freedom for those who believe. And Paul declares that this glorious, liberating truth will be testified to in due time. In other words, eventually, the news is going to get out.

And even today, we must keep this in mind: the testimony of Jesus Christ is not just a private story—it's public truth. The ransom He paid, the sacrifice He gave, and the mediation He provides—although there are those who would like to suppress or discount it—eventually, they will find it cannot be contained. The news is too good, too costly, and too powerful to stay silent.

In other words, you can try to suppress it, silence it, ignore it, or deny it—but eventually, the news is going to get out. And thank God, for many of us, it already has.

Isaiah foresaw it: "The earth shall be filled with the knowledge of the glory of the Lord as the waters cover the sea" (Isa. 11:9).

Jesus Himself said it: "And this gospel of the kingdom shall be preached in all the world... and then shall the end come" (Matt. 24:14).

Throughout history, there have always been voices that attempted to suppress, silence, or conceal the good news of the Gospel. Rome sought to stifle its spread. Religious leaders like the Pharisees endeavored to bury the truth. Even the grave itself tried to restrain its power. Yet, despite every effort, the message could not be contained—eventually, those voices were silenced, and the news emerged: He is risen!

Let me pause here to remind you of something that came to mind with that last thought: we live in a world full of voices, but not all voices tell the truth. In the cacophony of modern culture—where lies are dressed as facts and opinions masquerade as wisdom—the truth of Christ's ransom still stands. Eventually, it will pierce through the noise. It will overcome the distortion. And it will reach the ears of those it was meant for—just in time.

This is why Paul urges the church to continue praying for all people. Why? Because God desires that all will come to the knowledge of truth. That's the will of God. And when we align with God's will in prayer, we become instruments in the spreading of that redemptive news.

1 John 5:14 reminds us, "If we ask anything according to His will, He hears us." So, the next time you pray for a loved one to be saved, a prodigal to return, or a hardened heart to soften—remember, you're testifying ahead of time. You're echoing the eternal truth that news of Jesus will reach every ear it's destined for.

But what about those who feel beyond reach?

I'm glad you asked. I'm reminded of a story that deeply moved me. A grandmother from San Diego felt a divine burden to reach an unlikely mission field—California's Death Row. While most people had written these men off as monsters or lost causes, she saw them as souls. So, she started writing letters—not to preach at them, but to love on them.

She shared stories about her dog, church happenings, and her town's hot-air balloon festival. Inmates wrote back about their prison yard routines and the nightly chaos behind the bars. They even exchanged trivia questions. This wasn't a gimmick. It was grace in motion.

One attorney, who had prosecuted some of the inmates, criticized her work, saying, "These people are beyond redemption." But she responded, "I don't believe that. Nobody is beyond God's reach."

Let that settle in your spirit: Nobody is beyond redemption... Nobody is beyond God's reach.

That's what I would suggest this chapter reminds us of: Jesus paid the ransom—for all. Even the worst. Even the least. Even the ones society forgets. And whether they hear it now or later... eventually, the news will get out.

That's why we must live as walking headlines of God's grace, proclaiming, "He gave Himself for me. He paid the price. I'm no longer hostage to my past—He set me free."

And if He set you free... Make sure someone else hears the news.

So, what does this mean for you today?

It means you are now a living press release of heaven. It means your story, your testimony, and your transformation are part of God's campaign to spread the news.

Don't stay silent when the news is this good. Don't downplay what Christ has done in you and for you. Don't delay the message when someone nearby needs it today. You never know whose soul is hanging in the balance, waiting for a word, a witness, or a whisper of hope.

Yes, eventually, the news will get out. But let God use you to help make it happen.

Shout it. Share it. Show it. Because someone's breakthrough may be waiting on your boldness.

Paul says Christ "gave Himself a ransom for all, to be testified in due time." In other words, the cross wasn't a whisper—it was a headline waiting for its release. The powers of darkness tried to smother it. The stone tried to seal it. The guards tried to secure it. But you can't keep this kind of news locked up.

And here's the beauty: when the news got out, it didn't just stay in Jerusalem. It spread to Judea, to Samaria, and to the uttermost parts of the earth. And now—it's on us.

And that's the word I leave you with: now it's on us. It's on us to testify to His goodness, on us to testify to the price He paid... The cross was His—but now, it's on us. The ransom was His—but now, it's on us. The resurrection was His—but now, it's on us.

The apostles carried the news in their time—now, it's on us.

The martyrs carried the news in their generation—now, it's on us.

The Church has carried the news across centuries—and now, it's on us.

It's on us to testify.

It's on us to proclaim.

It's on us to embrace the testimony of Jesus Christ and spread the news that cannot be contained.

Because eventually, the news is going to get out. The only question is—will it get out through us?

LIVING THE LESSON

Throughout the week, take time to put into practice what you've read and reflected on. Each daily activity offers an opportunity to deepen your faith and live out the lessons from this devotional. On the following pages, engage with these activities to grow spiritually and strengthen your relationship with God and others.

Monday | Scripture Focus & Reflection

Begin your week meditating on the power of Christ's ransom and the truth that His sacrifice will one day be made known to all.

- 1 Timothy 2:5–6
- Hosea 13:14
- 2 Peter 3:9

Reflection Questions:

- What does it mean to you personally that Jesus paid a ransom for *you*?
- Have you ever taken the good news of the gospel for granted?
- What emotions rise in your heart when you realize you received the message *in time*?

Journaling Prompt:

Write a personal reflection on the moment you first understood Christ paid the ransom for your soul. What has changed in your life since then? How has the gospel become more real to you over time?

_____

_____

_____

_____

_____

_____

_____

_____

_____

_____

_____

Tuesday | Personal Prayer & Petition

Set aside intentional time to thank Jesus for His redemptive sacrifice and to pray for those who have not yet received the news.

Prayer Focus:

- Thank God that you heard the gospel before it was too late.
- Ask God to use you as a vessel to help spread the good news of Christ's redemption.
- Petition for the salvation of those still bound, whether physically, mentally, or spiritually.

Journaling Prompt:

Are there people in your life who you feel are "beyond redemption"? Bring their names before God in prayer. Ask Him to soften your heart and use you to reflect His love and truth to them.

_____

_____

_____

_____

_____

_____

_____

_____

_____

_____

_____

_____

_____

_____

_____

_____

_____

Wednesday | Midweek Worship & Gratitude

Let your worship overflow with gratitude that you are not beyond redemption, and that Jesus willingly paid the ransom for your life.

Worship Song Suggestions:

- "Thank You Jesus for the Blood" – Charity Gayle
- "The Blood Will Never Lose Its Power" – Andraé Crouch
- "He Paid It All" – Wess Morgan

Gratitude List:

- List 3 ways Christ's ransom has changed your life.
- Write a thank-you letter to Jesus, expressing your deep appreciation that you heard and received the gospel before it was too late.

_____

_____

_____

_____

_____

_____

_____

_____

_____

_____

_____

_____

_____

_____

_____

_____

Thursday | Outreach & Encouragement

Share the redeeming message of Christ with someone who needs hope today—remind them they are not too far gone.

Outreach Ideas:

- Share 1 Timothy 2:5–6 with someone and explain what the word "ransom" means spiritually.
- Write a note, card, or social media post offering hope to someone who feels unworthy of God's love.
- Tell a personal testimony of how God reached you when others may have counted you out.

Journaling Prompt:

Who in your life has yet to hear or fully receive the message of Christ's sacrifice? Write about how you can be intentional this week in testifying to them.

_____
_____
_____
_____
_____
_____
_____
_____
_____
_____
_____
_____
_____
_____
_____

Friday | Self-Examination & Recommitment

Today, reflect on the gravity of Christ's ransom and recommit yourself to living in a way that honors that great price.

Reflection Questions:

- Have I lived with the urgency that others still need to hear the gospel?
- What distractions or excuses have kept me from sharing the message?
- How can I honor Christ's ransom through my daily choices and relationships?

Journaling Prompt:

Write down any ways you've allowed comfort, fear, or doubt to keep you silent about your faith. Recommit today to being a living testimony that the ransom Jesus paid was not in vain.

_____
_____
_____
_____
_____
_____
_____
_____
_____
_____
_____
_____
_____
_____

Saturday & Sunday | Family Activity & Reflection

Use this weekend to reflect as a family on the power of redemption and how the good news is meant to be shared.

Group Discussion Ideas:

- Talk about what the word "ransom" means and how it applies to Jesus' sacrifice.
- Read 1 Timothy 2:5–6 together and discuss why the world still needs to hear this message.
- Ask each person to share how they first heard about Jesus, and what that moment meant to them.

Weekend Reflection:

As a family, create a *Testimony Time Capsule*. Write letters about how you each came to know Christ. Seal them in an envelope to read in the future. Pray together, thanking God that the news got to *you*, and ask Him to use your family to help spread it to others.

_____

_____

_____

_____

_____

_____

_____

_____

_____

_____

_____

_____

_____

_____

THAT'S A GOOD THING

It is good that a man should both hope and quietly wait for the salvation of the Lord.

LAMENTATIONS 3:26 (KJV)

"Every little bit helps."

———

We've all heard the saying, "Every little bit helps." It's one of those deceptively simple sayings that carries both practical wisdom and spiritual insight—a phrase that reminds us that even small acts of generosity, faith, or patience can make a significant difference. Like dropping coins into a jar each day, it doesn't feel like much at the time, but over time it becomes a savings account, an emergency fund, or even a blessing for someone in need.

A single push-up doesn't build strength, but doing a few daily can change the condition of one's body and health. One person volunteering for a few hours may seem small, but when many do it, lives are transformed, neighborhoods are renewed, and movements are born.

And let us not forget, reading one verse a day can birth a hunger for the whole Word. It's more than a catchy saying—it's a truth that resonates deeply in life and faith.

Biblically, I am reminded of the widow's two mites (Mark 12:41–44), where Jesus praised her "little" offering as greater than all the rest, because in God's economy, small sacrifices hold eternal weight.

Then there was the little boy's lunch (John 6:9), which accounted for just five loaves and two fish—not enough in human eyes. But in the hands of Jesus, it fed thousands. The lesson is clear: every little bit helps when surrendered to Him.

The point is this: God tends to multiply what we surrender, no matter how small. He notices every act of kindness, every quiet prayer, every "cup of cold water" given in His name.

I recall such a moment that left an impression on me. I was at a gas station when a young man approached me, visibly flustered. He explained that his car had sputtered to a stop just within sight of the pump. "Sir, I don't want to bother you, but anything would help," he said, motioning toward the vehicle. I saw his sincerity and the humility in his tone. I gave him $20—more than what was needed to get a few gallons of gas.

His eyes filled with gratitude. That experience reminded me of how God responds to our cries for help—not with the bare minimum, but with abundance.

That's the nature of divine help. Ephesians 3:20 tells us that God does "exceedingly and abundantly above all that we ask or think," but there's a condition: it happens "according to the power that works in us." And what is that power? It's hope.

The writer of Lamentations says it clearly: "It is good that a man should both hope and quietly wait for the salvation of the Lord." The Hebrew word for "good" here implies something beneficial, beautiful, and bountiful. In other words, this isn't just a "good idea"—this is God's idea. It's healthy for the soul, strengthening for the spirit, and transformational for your life to wait with hopeful expectation for God's help.

This is not sitting back passively with folded arms; to the contrary, it's leaning forward in faith, anticipating God's move. This hope is not wishful thinking; it's a confident assurance rooted in God's character and covenant.

And the irony is, hope isn't loud. It doesn't always come with a shout. Sometimes, it whispers, "Hold on just a little longer." Psalm 39:7 echoes this quiet resolve: "And now, Lord, what do I wait for? My hope is in You."

And let's be honest, waiting quietly is not always easy. When things concern us, we want answers fast, breakthroughs now, and solutions today. But spiritual growth happens in the waiting. I'll say that again:: spiritual growth happens in the waiting.

Isaiah 40:31 assures us "They that wait upon the Lord shall renew their strength." It's in that quiet waiting that strength is formed and faith is refined.

It's what gives you the strength to keep going when everything around you is trying to convince you to give up. For the psalmist in Psalm 119:81, it was the Word of God that provided that strength: "My soul faints for Your salvation, but I hope in Your Word."

For us, it's often a mix of things: a Scripture remembered, a prayer whispered in the dark, or the gentle encouragement of someone who reminds us that even in the delay, God is still working.

We hope in His Word, and we rest in His grace. As Paul wrote in 2 Thessalonians 2:16, God has given us "everlasting consolation and good hope by grace." Night always feels longest just before sunrise. But the sunrise always comes. Waiting with hope is believing the light is already on its way, and that should provide consolation. It should provide needed relief and reassurance, as well as encouragement.

This becomes crucial when we look at the fact that we live in a world where people are desperate for help—either financial, emotional, or spiritual.

Some turn to social media, self-help gurus, substances, or distractions, hoping to ease the ache. But those are examples of misplaced hope, and misplaced hope can lead to deeper disappointment. That's why Romans 5:5 declares, "Hope does not disappoint, because the love of God has been poured out in our hearts by the Holy Spirit."

Hope anchored and rooted in God is not misplaced hope. It's not wishful thinking—it's foundational trust.

The tragic crash of John F. Kennedy Jr.'s plane in 1999 serves as a sobering example of the contrast between misplaced hope and anchored hope. Though a licensed pilot, he wasn't certified to fly using instruments alone. On the night of the fatal accident, heavy fog obscured the sky, disorienting him. Without the ability to rely on visual cues, he likely experienced what pilots call "spatial disorientation"—where up feels like down and left feels like right. He trusted his instincts instead of the plane's instruments, and the result was fatal.

The spiritual parallel is profound. When life's circumstances grow foggy, and you can't see your way clearly, the temptation is to lean on your feelings. But feelings lie. Faith, however, calls you to trust the spiritual instruments God has placed before you: His Word, His promises, and His Spirit.

If you've ever felt lost in the fog of uncertainty, pain, or pressure, know this: God has given you what you need to navigate. Like a well-trained pilot, trust the instruments. Let hope serve as your compass and grace as your map.

As our Spiritual Vitamin suggests, "That's a Good Thing." Jeremiah says, "It is good that a man should both hope and quietly wait for the salvation of the Lord." He wrote those words in the middle of devastation, when everything around him looked hopeless. And yet—he chose to wait with expectation.

From a kingdom perspective, waiting without hope is torture. But waiting with hope is strength. It's like a seed in the ground—it may look buried, but in reality, it's planted. In other words, something is happening beneath the soil that you can't see. Just because you can't see growth doesn't mean it isn't happening. Waiting in faith is trusting what God is cultivating beneath the surface.

When you wait with hopeful expectation, you declare, "I may not be able to see that God has moved yet, but my expectation is that He will. Just like the night may still be dark, but the expectation is that morning is on the way."

Even when my strength may be weak, I am renewed with expectancy because His mercies are new every morning. So, what does it look like to embrace this quiet hope?

- It looks like praying when you don't know what else to do.
- It looks like worshiping when you're still waiting on your breakthrough.
- It looks like smiling through your tears and saying, "God's got me."
- It looks like trusting His plan, even when His pace doesn't match yours.

Every little act of faith matters. Every whispered prayer. Every Scripture recited. Every moment you choose to trust instead of panic. Every time you decide to believe in spite of what you see...that's a good thing.

Listen, you may not be where you want to be, but thank God you're not where you used to be. Keep hoping. Keep waiting. Keep believing. Because your quiet trust in God isn't wasted—it's working. That's not just a good idea...

That's a good thing.

LIVING THE LESSON

Throughout the week, take time to put into practice what you've read and reflected on. Each daily activity offers an opportunity to deepen your faith and live out the lessons from this devotional. On the following pages, engage with these activities to grow spiritually and strengthen your relationship with God and others.

Monday | Scripture Focus & Reflection

Start your week by anchoring your heart in the truth that even the smallest measure of hope, when rooted in God, is powerful and pleasing to Him.

- Lamentations 3:26
- Psalm 39:7
- 2 Thessalonians 2:16
- Psalm 46:1

Reflection Questions:

- What does it mean to you that it's "good" to hope and quietly wait on the Lord?
- Are you quietly waiting—or anxiously striving—for God's help?
- How has hope, even in small doses, sustained you in the past?

Journaling Prompt:

Reflect on a time when you clung to hope, even just a little, and God came through. How did your faith grow during that waiting season?

_____
_____
_____
_____
_____
_____
_____
_____
_____
_____

Tuesday | Personal Prayer & Petition

Today, offer God your honest prayers, whether full of faith or struggling to hope. Ask Him to increase your trust in His timing and guidance.

Prayer Focus:

- Thank God for being a present help, even when you can't see your way forward.
- Ask Him to strengthen your faith to trust His "spiritual instruments"—His Word and grace.
- Petition for peace as you wait quietly, knowing that waiting is not weakness, but worship.

Journaling Prompt:

What "fog" are you facing in your life right now? Where do you need to lean more into faith than feelings? Write out a prayer for clarity and peace in the wait.

_____

_____

_____

_____

_____

_____

_____

_____

_____

_____

_____

_____

_____

_____

Wednesday | Midweek Worship & Gratitude

Let your worship today rise from a place of gratitude, not for immediate answers, but for the *presence* of God in the waiting.

Worship Song Suggestions:

- "Wait on the Lord" – Maverick City Music ft. Chandler Moore
- "Trust in You" – Anthony Brown & group therAPy
- "Still" – Hillsong Worship

Gratitude List:

- List 3 things you're still hoping for, and thank God *in advance* for each outcome.
- Write a short note of gratitude to God for the moments when He came through quietly, but powerfully.

_____

_____

_____

_____

_____

_____

_____

_____

_____

_____

_____

_____

_____

_____

_____

_____

Thursday | Outreach & Encouragement

Be a voice of steady hope today. Encourage someone who may be navigating spiritual fog or feeling stuck while waiting.

Outreach Ideas:

- Text someone Lamentations 3:26 with a note that says, "Waiting on God is not wasted time."
- Share the story of JFK Jr.'s plane crash and how it reminds us to trust our "spiritual instruments."
- Reach out to a friend or family member who's in a holding pattern; offer to pray with them for renewed hope.

Journaling Prompt:

Who do you know that's in a foggy season right now? How can you gently encourage them to trust God's direction, even when it's unclear?

_____
_____
_____
_____
_____
_____
_____
_____
_____
_____
_____
_____
_____
_____
_____

Friday | Self-Examination & Recommitment

Pause to assess how you've been waiting. Is your hope active or passive? Recommit to trusting God not only with outcomes, but also with His process.

Reflection Questions:

- Have I been quietly hopeful or quietly resentful in this season?
- What spiritual "instruments" am I ignoring or misreading?
- How can I realign my hope with God's Word and grace today?

Journal Prompt:

Identify one area where you've been tempted to give up hope. What would it look like to trust again—even with just a small spark of belief? Write a declaration of faith to speak over that area.

_____
_____
_____
_____
_____
_____
_____
_____
_____
_____
_____
_____
_____
_____
_____

Saturday & Sunday | Family Activity & Reflection

This weekend, gather your family or close friends to reflect on the power of quiet, persistent hope, especially when life gets foggy.

Group Discussion Ideas:

- Read Lamentations 3:26 aloud and share what it means to each person.
- Share stories about times you waited on God and saw His hand move.
- Talk about areas in your lives where you are each still waiting and hoping.

Weekend Reflection:

As a group or family, create a "Hope Jar." Each person writes one hope or prayer they're quietly believing in God for. Place the slips in a jar and commit to praying over them weekly. Close with a time of prayer, asking God to help you trust His Word and timing, even when visibility is low.

_____

_____

_____

_____

_____

_____

_____

_____

_____

_____

_____

_____

VICTORY IS STILL ON THE TABLE

Rejoicing in hope; patient in tribulation; continuing instant in prayer.

ROMANS 12:12 (KJV)

"Victory begins with hope."

Hope is the seedbed of every spiritual victory. Our Spiritual Vitamin reminds us that, even when circumstances are stacked against us, we are called to rejoice in hope, be patient in tribulation, and stay persistent in prayer. This isn't just poetic language; to the contrary, it's a powerful progression of posture. When the storms rage, when uncertainty clouds your direction, when pressure surrounds you—don't lose your hope. Because hope is the spiritual cue that victory is still on the table.

Hope is not wishful thinking—it is confident expectation in God's promises. Hebrews 6:19 calls it "an anchor for the soul." Even if the winds of tribulation blow, hope keeps us from drifting.

As long as God is alive, as long as His promises stand, and as long as Jesus' tomb is empty, victory is never off the table. Hope guarantees there's still something to look forward to. In other words, no matter how dark the present looks, hope means the story isn't finished. The outcome isn't decided, and God is still at work.

Hope isn't a wish; it's an anchor. Hebrews 6:19 says, "We have this hope as an anchor for the soul, firm and secure." That means when the winds blow, when disappointment knocks at the door, when prayers seem unanswered—hope holds you steady.

The Apostle Paul's charge is simple yet profound: Don't let hardship drown your joy. Don't let adversity steal your patience. And don't let delay interrupt your devotion. Why? Because no situation that a believer encounters is truly hopeless. No matter how deep the valley, how high the mountain, or how long the night—hope remains, and victory is still on the table.

Like the football team that finds itself down at halftime, although they may look defeated, the game isn't over. As long as there's time on the clock, victory is still on the table. Such is the case in the game of life: you may find yourself down, but know you are never defeated, because Hope says, "Victory is still on the table...because of whose team we are on."

Speaking of sports, I'm reminded of a pivotal sports moment that carries a spiritual lesson. Back in the early days of his career, local boxing phenom Sugar Ray Leonard finally earned his shot at the welterweight crown. His opponent? The feared and ferocious Roberto Duran—a brawler with a reputation for punishment and power. Nicknamed "Manos de Piedra," or "Stone Hands," Duran was widely considered unbeatable and feared in the ranks of boxing.

In their first bout, Sugar Ray entered the ring not focused on his own ability, but on Duran's legend. He respected the opponent, but he feared him too. The fight went the distance, but Sugar Ray lost—not because he lacked skill, but because he lacked expectation. He came prepared to fight—but not prepared to win. In this life, we must not only come prepared to fight the good fight of faith but also come prepared to win.

In their rematch, everything changed. Sugar Ray danced. He smiled. He even mocked Duran in the ring. And then, to everyone's astonishment, Duran quit mid-fight, saying those infamous words: "No más." What changed? His conditioning? No. His strategy? Maybe slightly. But the real difference was his mindset. This time, he came prepared and expected to win.

The same is true in life and faith. Many believers lose not because they lack the ability, but because they lack the belief. You must learn to see yourself as a victor before the fight even begins.

Paul warns that after the initial high of salvation, many slip into a lukewarm faith—a spiritual fatigue that settles in when fervor fades. It's why he says in the verses surrounding our Scripture focus, "Be not slothful in business; be fervent in spirit; serve the Lord" (Romans 12:11).

That word "fervent" means boiling over—alive, intense, passionate. It's the same kind of fire that burned in Apollos (Acts 18:25) and the same fire that was missing from the Laodicean church, whom Jesus rebuked for being "neither hot nor cold" (Revelation 3:15–16).

Let's be clear: this walk of faith requires heat. You can't win battles with cold faith. You won't move mountains with lukewarm belief. Victory requires more than attendance—it demands expectation. You must not only show up; you must believe that something favorable will happen.

"Against all hope, Abraham in hope believed…" (Romans 4:18). Though old and childless, victory was still on the table because God had spoken.

Joseph was sold as a slave, thrown in prison, and forgotten (Genesis 50:20), yet victory was still on the table. What men meant for evil, God turned for good.

And to the disciples in Luke 24—the cross on that Friday looked like the end. Saturday was silent. But Sunday morning proved victory was still on the table.

Hope says the chapter isn't the conclusion. Hope declares that if God is still on the throne, victory is still on the table. And if we can buy into this belief, then Paul says in our Spiritual Vitamin that we should be "Rejoicing in Hope." Let's break the three down before us for clarity and insight:

Paul tells us to "rejoice in hope." "Rejoicing in hope" means maintaining an inner celebration even before the situation changes. It's praising in advance. It's dancing while still in the valley. That means no matter what life looks like, we don't rejoice in the pain; we rejoice in the promise. We don't rejoice in the trial; we rejoice in the triumph that's coming.

Rejoicing in hope is saying, "Yes, I'm in a battle, but victory is still on the table. Yes, I'm in a storm, but deliverance is still on the table. Yes, I may be down right now, but my God specializes in comebacks, and as long as He's alive, victory is never off the table."

Abraham believed it. Joseph lived it. The cross confirmed it. And we can stand on it: victory is still on the table when we rejoice in hope.

But then he tells us to be "patient in tribulation," which means enduring without collapsing, staying steady when life gets stormy. He doesn't say tribulation won't come. He doesn't say believers are exempt from storms, losses, or suffering. What he says is—when trouble comes, hold your ground. Don't break. Don't give up. Don't let the fire of tribulation extinguish the flame of your faith.

Patience in tribulation means endurance under pressure. It means standing steady when the weight is heavy. It means trusting that God is working even when nothing seems to be moving.

Shadrach, Meshach, and Abednego were patient in the fire—and they discovered a fourth man walking with them. Job was patient in tribulation—and in the end, God gave him double for his trouble. Paul himself was beaten, shipwrecked, and imprisoned, yet he was patient in tribulation, and the gospel spread all over the world.

Patience in tribulation is not passive waiting—it's active endurance. It's declaring, "This won't break me, this will build me. This won't defeat me; this will develop me. This won't stop me; this will strengthen me."

And finally, Paul closes the verse by saying, "continuing instant in prayer." In other words—stay connected. Because prayer is not our last resort; it is our first response.

To "continue" in prayer means we don't quit just because the answer hasn't come yet. We pray until something shifts. We pray until God moves. We pray until peace floods our hearts.

To be "instant" in prayer means to stay on call—like a soldier ready for orders or a doctor on duty. At any moment, in any place, under any pressure, the believer has one reflex: prayer. Whether in the valley or on the mountaintop, in the midnight hour or at the break of day, prayer is always the posture.

Daniel was instant in prayer when he opened his window toward Jerusalem three times a day, even when it could cost him his life. Jesus was instant in prayer when He went to Gethsemane and poured His soul out before the Father. The early church was instant in prayer when Peter was locked in prison—and God sent an angel to open the doors.

Continuing instant in prayer means this: when you can't work it out, you can still pray it through. When you don't have the answer, you know the One who does. When nothing else seems possible, prayer keeps you connected to the God for whom nothing is impossible.

So, keep praying. Pray when you're weary. Pray when you're waiting. Pray when you're winning. Stay instant, stay ready, stay connected —because prayer is the line that keeps heaven open over your life.

To "continue instant in prayer" means never letting go of your lifeline. When the wait is long, the answer feels delayed, and the pressure mounts—pray instantly, persistently, and expectantly.

And so, at the end of the day, know this: you are not fighting for victory—you are fighting from victory. Jesus has already overcome the world, and you are more than a conqueror through Him (Romans 8:37). So hold your head high, square your shoulders, rejoice, be patient, keep praying, and know, "Victory is still on the table."

- You may be surrounded, but it's still on the table.
- You may be outnumbered, but it's still on the table.

- \You may be weary, but it's still on the table.

If God is for you, who can be against you? So, shift your language from defeat to destiny. Start saying what you expect, not just what you see. Don't say, "I hope it works out." Say, "I know God is working it out." Speak like someone who knows the tomb is empty and the throne is still occupied.

Train your spirit to respond to trials with faith, not fear. Let worship be your weapon and truth be your target. Because when you expect to win, every setback becomes a setup, every test becomes a testimony, and every struggle becomes a stage for God's glory. Remember, this fight isn't final. This test isn't terminal. And our God isn't finished.

The secret weapon of victorious believers has never been muscle or intellect—it's hope. A hope that sees beyond the present pain. A hope that clings to the promise. And a hope that wakes up each morning expecting something to change, because with the dawning of each new day comes the realization that "Victory is still on the table."

LIVING THE LESSON

Throughout the week, take time to put into practice what you've read and reflected on. Each daily activity offers an opportunity to deepen your faith and live out the lessons from this devotional. On the following pages, engage with these activities to grow spiritually and strengthen your relationship with God and others.

Monday | Scripture Focus & Reflection

Let today be a moment of realignment. Refocus your heart on God's promise that hope is the anchor for every trial, and victory begins with the right mindset.

- Romans 12:12
- Acts 18:25
- Revelation 3:15–16
- 1 Corinthians 15:57

Reflection Questions:

- How does your perspective shape your experience in trials?
- Have you been expecting defeat or declaring victory in advance?
- What does it mean to "rejoice in hope" when things don't look hopeful?

Journal Prompt:

Write about a situation where you lost before the battle even began because of your mindset. Then, write a declaration reversing that mentality with hope and faith.

_____
_____
_____
_____
_____
_____
_____
_____
_____
_____

Tuesday | Personal Prayer & Petition

In today's prayer time, lay your battles before the Lord, but with expectation. Ask God to renew your mind so that you enter every challenge with victorious hope.

Prayer Focus:

- Ask God to shift your perspective from defeat to victory.
- Pray for a mindset that reflects heaven's assurance, not earth's circumstances.
- Invite the Holy Spirit to stir up fervency and spiritual passion.

Journal Prompt:

List one battle you are currently facing. Pray over it, then write a short letter to yourself declaring: "I expect to win because my hope is in God."

_____
_____
_____
_____
_____
_____
_____
_____
_____
_____
_____
_____
_____
_____

Wednesday | Midweek Worship & Gratitude

SWorship isn't just what you do when you win, it's *how* you win. Let your midweek praise reflect the joy of a heart already claiming victory.

Worship Song Suggestions:

- "Victory" – Tye Tribbett
- "Expecting Great Things" – Jonathan Nelson
- "More Than Conquerors" – Rend Collective

Gratitude List:

- List five things you've already overcome that seemed impossible.
- Thank God for the unseen victories currently in motion on your behalf.

_____
_____
_____
_____
_____
_____
_____
_____
_____
_____
_____
_____
_____
_____
_____
_____
_____
_____
_____

Thursday | Outreach & Encouragement

Victory is contagious. Speak life into someone else today and remind them that they, too, can expect to win, even if they feel like they're losing.

Outreach Ideas:

- Call or text someone who's discouraged and remind them: "Victory begins with hope."
- Share the story of Sugar Ray Leonard's mindset shift on social media or in a group chat.
- Send Romans 12:12 to someone who needs strength for the battle they're in.

Journal Prompt:

Who in your circle is facing a tough fight right now? How can your hope become their encouragement today?

_____
_____
_____
_____
_____
_____
_____
_____
_____
_____
_____
_____
_____
_____

Friday | Self-Examination & Recommitment

Today, do an honest check: Have you been fighting from a place of fear or faith? Let the Word reset your posture as you recommit to victory thinking.

Reflection Questions:

- What thoughts or habits have kept me spiritually "lukewarm"?
- Where have I lost fervor and forgotten that I'm fighting from victory, not for it?
- What would it look like to show up with a mindset that expects to win?

Journal Prompt:

Write a *victory creed*—a short declaration that affirms your identity as more than a conqueror and reminds you that hope is your battle strategy.

_____

_____

_____

_____

_____

_____

_____

_____

_____

_____

_____

_____

_____

_____

Saturday & Sunday | Family Activity & Reflection

This weekend, gather your family or close friends for a discussion about mindset and victory. Use this time to sow seeds of faith into one another.

Group Discussion Ideas:

- Read Romans 12:12 aloud together. What does each phrase mean to you personally?
- Share one area where each person needs to adopt a "victory mindset."
- Discuss the Sugar Ray Leonard story and how a shift in expectation changed the outcome.

Weekend Reflection:

Create a "Victory Wall" in your home. Write down current challenges on sticky notes, but label each one with a faith-filled declaration like: *"I expect to win."* Let it serve as a visual reminder that no matter the battle, your mindset is grounded in hope.

_____
_____
_____
_____
_____
_____
_____
_____
_____
_____
_____
_____

STAND ON FAITH

And there sat a certain man at Lystra, impotent in his feet, being a cripple from his mother's womb, who never had walked: The same heard Paul speak: who stedfastly beholding him, and perceiving that he had faith to be healed, Said with a loud voice, Stand upright on thy feet. And he leaped and walked.

ACTS 14:8–10 (KJV)

"I've got faith that's good enough to stand on."

In our Spiritual Vitamin, Paul notices a poor soul—a man whose feet had never worked, crippled from birth. He was living with what today we'd call a pre-existing condition. It's a phrase familiar to many, especially in healthcare debates, where insurance companies once had the liberty to deny coverage for conditions that existed before the start of a policy. In other words, if you were already sick when you signed up, too bad—they wouldn't pay for your healing.

But thank God that in the economy of grace, we're not denied coverage because of our pre-existing conditions! Sin left us with a spiritual condition we were born into, yet God extended full coverage through the finished work of Christ. We don't need a co-pay, we don't have to wait for approval, and there's no deductible—because Jesus paid it all!

Romans 3:23 reminds us, "All have sinned, and come short of the glory of God." That's the spiritual diagnosis. But thankfully, our prognosis isn't hopeless. Isaiah 53:5 declares, "By His stripes we are healed." Healing, deliverance, restoration—it's all included in the benefit package of salvation.

In our Spiritual Vitamin, the Apostle Paul is preaching, and in the middle of his message, he not only notices this individual, but he also sees something in this man's eyes: faith to be healed. This man had never walked a day in his life. Not a temporary injury, not a passing weakness—but a lifelong pre-existing condition.

The text says Paul was "steadfastly beholding him." In other words, Paul didn't just glance—he gazed. He looked deeper than the surface. He saw beyond the crippled feet and into the condition of the man's heart. And what did he see? Faith.

This man had "faith to be healed." Faith doesn't always show up in shouts or tears—it often hides in attentive listening, in quiet expectation, in that subtle nod that says, "I believe this might be for me." Paul saw it. And he spoke with authority to it: "Stand upright on thy feet!"

That command wasn't just about posture—it was a call to faith. A spiritual challenge to move from paralysis to purpose. This man didn't stand on positive vibes or good intentions; rather, his faith was anchored in the Word he heard being preached (Romans 10:17: "Faith comes by hearing, and hearing by the word of God.").

At the end of the day, faith must have a foundation, and that foundation is God's Word. Because of what this man heard, he saw that his pre-existing condition wasn't his conclusion.

So many people today live spiritually crippled by their past, by trauma, by fear, by repeated failure, because they believe their condition is their conclusion. They sit—impotent in their faith—thinking they'll never walk into a new season.

But here's the truth: Your condition is not your conclusion. You might have a pre-existing condition—an addiction, a failed marriage, a broken trust, a lost opportunity—but it doesn't disqualify you from walking again into a sense of purpose and fulfillment. In fact, those very places of brokenness can become platforms for the miraculous when touched by faith.

1 John 1:9 gives us assurance: "If we confess our sins, He is faithful and just to forgive us and cleanse us from all unrighteousness." Here is the most important thing to remember: our faith isn't in our ability to stand—it's in God's power to raise us up. And He uses His Word to accomplish that objective, because He wants us to learn to appreciate the fact that we can stand on His Word.

Sometimes, faith doesn't start with a shout or a march. Sometimes, it finds you sitting in places of disappointment. It finds you in pews, in hospital beds, at kitchen tables, or in the stillness of the midnight hour. It finds you where you are and invites you into where you're destined to be, and all you must do is stand on His Word.

This man at Lystra wasn't asking to be healed. He was simply present and listening. And that was enough. Presence with expectation is the seedbed for the miraculous.

Acts 14 shows us a man who had never stood before, yet in one moment of faith he not only stood, he leaped and walked. That's what I call faith to stand on.

Faith is not built on feelings—it's built on the Word of God. When Paul preached, this man heard something that gave him the courage to believe the impossible. And Paul didn't lift him. Paul didn't push him. Paul just gave him a Word to stand on.

Faith to stand on is what carries you when life has crippled you. It's what lifts you when circumstances have held you down. It's what empowers you to do what you've never done before.

So, hear me: you may have been down your whole life, but faith says you don't have to stay there. You may have never walked in freedom, never stood in confidence, never moved in victory—but faith says today can be the day. All it takes is one word from God, one act of obedience, and you'll discover what it means to have faith to stand on.

There comes a time when you can no longer sit in your condition, pre-existing or otherwise. You've heard the Word. You've listened long enough. Now it's time to get up. Paul didn't offer the man a gradual healing process—he spoke a direct word: "Stand upright! " The man didn't hesitate, didn't ask for proof—he leaped and walked. Why? Because faith responded to the command.

Here's the principle: faith doesn't sit around waiting for convenience. It moves, even when conditions haven't changed yet. Faith believes that just one word from God is enough.

Peter and John in Acts 3 told the lame man at the gate called Beautiful to "rise up and walk," and he leapt, stood, and entered the temple walking and praising. Peter stepped out of the boat in Matthew 14:29 and "stood on water" because his faith was anchored in Jesus' word, "Come."

Whether it was the lame man rising to walk or Peter stepping out on the water, both remind us that when faith is anchored in the Word of Jesus, what was once impossible becomes the very ground we can stand on. So let me ask you today—in what area of your life is God calling you to take a stand on His Word? What is God commanding you to stand up from and for?

Are you being crippled by comparisons, paralyzed by shame, sitting in bitterness, or stalled in fear? Then it's time to stand. Stand up on His promises. Stand up on your purpose. Stand up on the testimony that's still being written.

Listen, there is something powerful about standing. In Scripture, standing often symbolizes readiness, strength, and spiritual authority. Ephesians 6:13 exhorts, "Having done all… to stand." To stand is to say, "I refuse to be identified by what I was born with, what I went through, or what I've lost."

You're not standing because you've never been knocked down. You're standing because God called you up! Paul's voice to that crippled man echoes through the ages: "Stand upright on thy feet." And I want to echo it today in your spirit. You've heard the Word. Now walk it out.

Don't just sit on your faith. Stand on it. Because if your faith is good enough to sit with, it's good enough to stand on.

LIVING THE LESSON

Throughout the week, take time to put into practice what you've read and reflected on. Each daily activity offers an opportunity to deepen your faith and live out the lessons from this devotional. On the following pages, engage with these activities to grow spiritually and strengthen your relationship with God and others.

Monday | Scripture Focus & Reflection

Start the week by letting your faith rise above your pre-existing conditions. Meditate on the truth that change is possible, and it begins with what you believe.

- Acts 14:8–10
- 2 Corinthians 5:21
- James 4:17
- 1 John 1:8–10
- 1 John 3:4

Reflection Questions:

- What "pre-existing condition" has kept you from standing fully in faith?
- Have you allowed past pain, sin, or failure to define your future?
- What would change in your life if you truly believed your faith was enough?

Journal Prompt:

Write about an area in your life where you feel stuck or "crippled." Then speak life over it by writing a faith declaration beginning with, *"I believe my condition can change because…"*

_____

_____

_____

_____

_____

_____

_____

_____

Tuesday | Personal Prayer & Petition

In prayer today, stop hiding behind past mistakes or present struggles. Talk to God honestly, and then boldly ask Him to empower your next step of faith.

Prayer Focus:

- Confess areas where you've accepted defeat instead of believing for healing or change.
- Ask God to help you *see* what He sees in you, just like Paul saw the man's faith.
- Pray for the courage to *stand up* in faith, even if your condition hasn't yet changed.

Journal Prompt:

Write a prayer asking God to help you live by faith and not by sight. Ask Him to strengthen your spiritual legs so you can stand.

Wednesday | Midweek Worship & Gratitude

Celebrate your future healing in advance. Worship like the man in Acts who leapt up and walked! Your praise is a sign that you already believe your breakthrough is coming.

Worship Song Suggestions:

- "I Believe" – Jonathan Nelson
- "Stand in Faith" – Danny Gokey
- "He Looked Beyond My Fault" – Gospel Hymn

Gratitude List:

- Thank God for covering your pre-existing spiritual conditions with grace.
- List 3 past situations where God helped you *stand up* again.
- Give thanks for one area of your life where you're believing for change.

_____
_____
_____
_____
_____
_____
_____
_____
_____
_____
_____
_____
_____
_____
_____
_____

Thursday | Outreach & Encouragement

Share your faith with someone who's struggling to stand. Be the voice that says, *"Stand upright on your feet!"*

Outreach Ideas:

- Reach out to someone with a past they think disqualifies them, and remind them God still has a future for them.
- Share Acts 14:8–10 in a text or on social media with a personal message: *"Your condition can change."*
- Encourage someone who's "waiting for an elevator" to start taking faith-filled steps instead.

Journal Prompt:

Who do you know that needs help believing in their own healing or breakthrough? What can you say to them today to spark their faith?

_____

_____

_____

_____

_____

_____

_____

_____

_____

_____

_____

_____

_____

_____

_____

_____

_____

Friday | Self-Examination & Recommitment

Pause to examine whether your faith is active or passive. Are you waiting for change, or believing for it?

Reflection Questions:

- What keeps you from fully believing that your condition can change?
- Have you taken action steps in faith, or are you waiting for things to be "perfect"?
- What would "standing on faith" look like for you this week?

Journaling Prompt:

Write a letter to yourself as if you were Paul, speaking to the crippled man. What would you say to encourage yourself to get up and walk?

_____

_____

_____

_____

_____

_____

_____

_____

_____

_____

_____

_____

_____

_____

_____

_____

_____

Saturday & Sunday | Family Activity & Reflection

Use the weekend to reflect with family or loved ones on how faith changes everything—even things we thought would never change.

Group Discussion Ideas:

- Read Acts 14:8–10 aloud and discuss what it means to "have faith to be healed."
- Talk about areas in your family history that may feel like "pre-existing conditions" (generational patterns, struggles, etc.) and speak declarations of healing over them.
- Share testimonies of times when faith brought unexpected change.

Weekend Reflection:

Invite each person to write down one condition they want God to change—physical, spiritual, emotional, or relational. Fold the papers and place them in a jar labeled *"Faith to Be Healed."* At the end of the month, return to the jar and see what God has done.

_____
_____
_____
_____
_____
_____
_____
_____
_____
_____
_____
_____

FLAWED FRUIT

Wherefore by their fruits ye shall know them.

MATTHEW 7:20 (KJV)

"You may be flawed, but you still have fruit."

To put it in proper context, Jesus is teaching about false prophets. He doesn't tell us to judge them by their appearance, charisma, or claims, but by their fruit. In other words, fruit reveals truth.

The real evidence of a life, a ministry, or a person's walk with God isn't found in appearance, charisma, or even words; but in their fruit. And here is the kingdom principle: fruit doesn't lie. A tree can wear leaves of pretense, but the fruit will tell the truth. Jesus cursed a fig tree because it appeared to be fruitful, but upon closer examination, it wasn't.

A person can polish their image, but their fruit will expose their character. Fruit is heaven's witness, the undeniable evidence of what's really at work in the roots of your life.

Fruit reveals its source; the kind of fruit a tree produces reveals the kind of tree it is. Apple trees don't grow oranges; thorns don't produce grapes. In the same way, the life we live reveals the condition of the heart. Character, conduct, and consistency will always expose the root. That's why Jesus said, "A good tree cannot bring forth evil fruit, neither can a corrupt tree bring forth good fruit." (Matt. 7:18)

You can fake an image for a season, but you can't fake fruit forever. But not only does fruit reveal its source, it also reveals health.

Fruit is a natural indicator of whether a tree is thriving or diseased. A tree may have leaves that look good, but if the fruit is bitter, rotten, or absent, it reveals something deeper. Spiritually, fruit exposes whether the soul is healthy. Galatians 5:22–23 describes the fruit of the Spirit—love, joy, peace, patience, kindness, goodness, faithfulness, gentleness, self-control. If those are missing, it reveals a disconnect at the root. In other words, fruit reveals whether we are walking in the Spirit or in the flesh.

Fruit also reveals maturity. It doesn't appear overnight; it comes as the tree grows, endures seasons, and draws from its roots. Likewise, spiritual fruit is the evidence of growth over time. It shows whether we are maturing in Christ or staying stagnant.

But this is what many of us overlook: fruit reveals legacy. Our fruit —our influence, our impact, our testimony—tells the truth about what we've invested in others. It shows whether our life points people to Christ or away from Him. And here is the takeaway: the fruit you bear today becomes the seed someone else plants tomorrow.

With that in mind, Jesus is pointing out attributes that flow from those who truly embrace Kingdom principles. He warns against being quick to judge, and He calls us to ask in faith, but always with the understanding that living in the fullness of Kingdom benefits is not easy. Why? Because it demands much of us. Remember, He was speaking to people whose flaws were so visible that they failed to discern the opportunity standing right before them in Christ.

Therefore, I would have you consider this thought: to live a fruitful

life in spite of our flaws, we must first be able to cultivate discernment
—the ability to recognize opportunities that come through a meaningful relationship with Jesus. In the Old Testament, five Hebrew
words are translated "discern," with the central idea being to observe
carefully. Proverbs 7:7 says, "And saw among the simple, I perceived
among the youths a young man devoid of understanding." Notice how
discernment and understanding walk hand in hand. Ecclesiastes 8:5
reinforces this truth: "A wise man's heart discerns both time and judgment." Wisdom and understanding are fruits from the same tree.

In the New Testament, three key Greek words—*anakrínō, diakrínō,*
and *dokimázō*—carry the idea of critical knowledge and spiritual
perception. Paul writes in 1 Corinthians 2:14: "The natural man does
not receive the things of the Spirit of God, for they are foolishness to
him; nor can he know them, because they are spiritually discerned."

Even Jesus rebuked those who could read the weather but missed
the deeper signs of God's activity, saying in Matthew 16:3, "You know
how to discern the face of the sky, but you cannot discern the signs of
the times."

Jesus said, "By their fruits you shall know them." Why? Because
fruit reveals truth. Fruit doesn't lie. It reveals source, it reveals health,
it reveals maturity, and it reveals legacy.

A tree can wear leaves of pretense, but the fruit will tell the truth.
A person can polish their image, but their fruit will expose their character. Fruit is heaven's witness—the undeniable evidence of what's
really at work in the roots of your life.

So don't just ask, "What does it look like? " Ask, "What fruit does
it bear?" Because in the end, fruit always reveals the truth.

In this Spiritual Vitamin, Jesus makes it clear: the way into the
Kingdom is through the narrow gate. That road is not easy—it
demands discipline, surrender, and self-denial. The broad path, on the
other hand, is wide open and feels comfortable, but it's deadly. Why?
Because it caters to our flaws, feeds our impulses, and leads to decisions that carry devastating consequences.

That's why Jesus issues a warning: "Beware of false prophets."
They'll point you toward the broad way. They'll sound convincing,

look harmless, and even dress like sheep—but beneath the surface, they're ravenous wolves.

Some of you ought to pause right here and thank God that He gave you discernment—that He opened your eyes to see truth. There was a time you may have admired the wrong people, even envied their so-called success. But now you recognize the truth: they had leaves without fruit. And as Jesus taught us, fruit is the real evidence. It tells the truth about a life—whether it's self-serving or God-glorifying.

Without discernment, you might still be entangled in relationships that drain you or chasing crowds that are going nowhere fast. But discernment doesn't just expose others—it reveals you. It holds up a mirror to your flaws and imperfections, while at the same time pointing you to Christ, who makes it possible to still be fruitful in spite of them.

Because here's some good news: flaws don't disqualify you from bearing fruit. In fact, it's often through the cracks that God's grace shines the brightest. And with discernment, you not only recognize what's fake around you, but you also embrace what's real within you —the fruit of a life rooted in Him.

There's a story about a house servant who carried two pots on a pole across his shoulders. One pot was perfect, while the other was cracked, leaking water along the path. For two years, the cracked pot delivered only half its load and felt ashamed of its flaw. One day, the pot apologized to the servant for its imperfection. The servant responded, "As we return to the master's house, look at the beautiful flowers along the path."

The pot noticed flowers growing only on its side of the path. The servant explained, "I've always known about your flaw, so I planted seeds along your side of the path. Every day, as we walk back, you water them. For two years, I've been able to pick these flowers to decorate my master's table."

Well, here is some more good news: we all have flaws, but God can use them to bring grace and beauty to His table. Through our relationship with Christ, we can be fruitful despite our imperfections.

The Apostle Paul is a powerful biblical example of this. He referred to his own flaw as a "thorn in the flesh"—something he prayed would be removed. Yet God's response was, "My grace is sufficient for you, for My strength is made perfect in weakness" (2 Corinthians 12:9). Paul's thorn did not disqualify him from being fruitful; it was the very thing God used to showcase His glory.

Even our spiritual heroes were not without faults. Moses struggled with anger. David committed adultery. and Peter denied Christ, yet each of them bore fruit that honored God.

Modern research from the Harvard Study of Adult Development— one of the longest studies on human flourishing—reveals something striking: people who embrace their imperfections and pursue authentic growth in spirit and character are the ones who live with the most resilience, compassion, and fruitfulness. That's not just psychology; that's Scripture. Paul declared, "My grace is sufficient for thee, for my strength is made perfect in weakness" (2 Cor. 12:9). In other words, what the world calls a flaw, God can turn into fertile ground for His strength to shine.

Consider Fanny Crosby, blind from infancy, yet the author of over 8,000 hymns. Her blindness—the very flaw many thought disqualified her—became the soil where her greatest fruit was planted. Out of her limitation came words that still give life to the church: *"Blessed Assurance, Jesus is mine."*

So, I encourage you today: let discernment be your guide. Not only to recognize the fruit—or the lack of fruit—in others, but also to recognize that your own flaws, when surrendered to Christ, are not wasted. They are the very places where His power produces fruit for His glory.

Because in the Kingdom of God, even flawed fruit is still fruit. And that fruit—born out of weakness, watered by grace, and ripened by faith—is the kind that brings honor to the Vine. So, let this be your declaration: "I may be flawed, but I still have fruit."

LIVING THE LESSON

Throughout the week, take time to put into practice what you've read and reflected on. Each daily activity offers an opportunity to deepen your faith and live out the lessons from this devotional. On the following pages, engage with these activities to grow spiritually and strengthen your relationship with God and others.

Monday | Scripture Focus & Reflection

Begin the week by reflecting on what it means to be fruitful, even in your flaws. Let the Word remind you that God sees beyond imperfections and uses them for His glory.

- Matthew 7:20
- Ecclesiastes 8:5
- Proverbs 7:7
- 1 Corinthians 2:14
- Matthew 16:3

Reflection Questions:

- In what ways has God brought fruit out of your flaws?
- Are there areas in your life where you're afraid your flaws disqualify you?
- How has discernment helped you avoid unfruitful paths?

Journal Prompt:

Write about one "cracked pot" area in your life and how God might be using it to water someone else's path.

_____
_____
_____
_____
_____
_____
_____
_____
_____
_____
_____

Tuesday | Personal Prayer & Petition

Approach God in honesty about your flaws today. Ask for increased discernment to see yourself and others clearly, and the grace to be fruitful despite your weaknesses.

Prayer Focus:

- Confess areas where you've judged others without fruit inspection.
- Ask God to open your eyes to spiritual truth and understanding.
- Pray for the wisdom to discern the difference between charisma and character.

Journal Prompt:

List any areas where your flaws have become excuses. Now write a prayer of surrender, asking God to use those same flaws for His glory.

_____
_____
_____
_____
_____
_____
_____
_____
_____
_____
_____
_____
_____
_____
_____

Wednesday | Midweek Worship & Gratitude

Give thanks today that God doesn't require perfection; He desires fruit. Worship Him for the ways He turns your imperfections into purpose.

Worship Song Suggestions:

- "Gracefully Broken" – Tasha Cobbs Leonard
- "Broken Things" – Matthew West
- "You Know My Name" – Tasha Cobbs Leonard ft. J. J. Hairston

Gratitude List:

- Thank God for using flawed people to do great things (like Moses, David, Peter).
- Reflect on a time when your weakness produced unexpected fruit.
- Thank God for people who saw the fruit in you despite your flaws.

_____

_____

_____

_____

_____

_____

_____

_____

_____

_____

_____

_____

Thursday | Outreach & Encouragement

Encourage someone today who feels disqualified by their imperfections. Be the voice that reminds them, "You may be flawed, but you still have fruit."

Outreach Ideas:

- Write or text a friend reminding them of the fruit you've seen in their life.
- Share the cracked pot story with someone who feels like they're not good enough.
- Post a message on social media: *"God uses cracked pots to water paths. Keep growing."*

Journaling Prompt:

Who in your life needs to hear that their flaws don't define them? How can you encourage them today?

_____
_____
_____
_____
_____
_____
_____
_____
_____
_____
_____
_____
_____
_____
_____

Friday | Self-Examination & Recommitment

It's time to check your own fruit. Not perfection, but evidence of spiritual growth. Be honest with yourself and ask: Am I growing?

Reflection Questions:

- What fruit is your life currently producing?
- Are you focused more on appearances than on impact?
- How is God inviting you to grow in discernment and depth?

Journal Prompt:

Make two lists: "Flaws I've surrendered" and "Fruit that came from them." Then recommit to letting God use every part of your story for His glory.

Saturday & Sunday | Family Activity & Reflection

Use the weekend to explore what it means to bear fruit as a family or group, even when no one is perfect.

Group Discussion Ideas:

- Read the cracked pot story aloud and discuss what each family member believes their "flawed area" might be.
- Share one thing you've seen God do through someone else's imperfections.
- Reflect on how discernment can help you choose the narrow path in daily life.

Weekend Reflection:

As a family or group, draw a tree and label each branch with a fruit of the Spirit (Galatians 5:22–23). Under each fruit, write ways you've seen that fruit growing in your home or relationships—even through hard seasons. Celebrate that flawed fruit is still fruit when it's surrendered to God.

_____
_____
_____
_____
_____
_____
_____
_____
_____
_____
_____
_____
_____

GET WITH THE PROGRAM

And for their sakes I sanctify myself, that they also might be sanctified through the truth.

JOHN 17:19 (KJV)

"Embrace God's truth to live a life set apart for His purpose and glory."

J ohn 17 is often called the "High Priestly Prayer." Jesus is hours away from the cross, and He's praying for His disciples—and for all who would come after them. Notice this: He isn't praying first for their comfort, their success, or even their safety. He prays for their sanctification in truth. Why? Because truth is what sets them apart, shapes them, and keeps them aligned with the Father's will in a hostile world. Truth will set you apart, shape your viewpoint, and keep you aligned with God's will for your life.

Mark Twain once said, "Never tell the truth to people who are not worthy of it." His words, though draped in wit, reveal a hard reality: many people would rather live comfortably in illusion than face the

cost of truth. Why? Because truth is confrontational. Truth has consequences. It doesn't just inform—it transforms. It disrupts the status
quo and challenges what has been comfortable for too long.

But Jesus doesn't shy away from truth. He declares, *"You shall know
the truth, and the truth shall make you free"* (John 8:32). The truth of
God's Word doesn't just set the record straight—it sets the captive
free. It releases us from deception, from mediocrity, from the chains of
past identity and worldly conformity. Truth isn't just an idea; it's a
person. Jesus said, *"I am the way, the truth, and the life"* (John 14:6).

In our Spiritual Vitamin, Jesus makes a profound declaration: *"For
their sakes, I sanctify myself."* At first glance, this may seem perplexing.
Wasn't Jesus already pure? Already holy? Yes—He was sinless and
fully sanctified in nature. But in this moment, He's making a
purposeful decision. He is choosing to fully consecrate Himself to
God's redemptive plan. Why? For our sake.

Jesus "got with the program." He submitted His will to the
Father's. He laid aside earthly comfort for eternal consequence. He
separated Himself—not in isolation, but in intention. And He did this
so that we too might be sanctified through the truth.

The power of truth is that it has the potential to sanctify. To sanctify means *"to set apart, to make holy, to dedicate."* Jesus says the instru-
ment God uses for this is truth. Not an opinion. Not popularity. Not
culture. Truth. And don't miss this: sanctification by truth isn't
optional—it's essential in God's providential design.

Sanctification by truth is not an accessory to faith; it's the essence
of faith. Not optional, but essential. Not a side choice, but the very
source of a set-apart life.

To be sanctified means to be set apart for sacred use. It doesn't
mean separated in superiority; it means aligned in purpose. In the Old
Testament, objects in the tabernacle were sanctified—not because they
were better than other items, but because they had a holy assignment.
In the same way, believers are called to live sanctified lives—not to
boast, but to be useful.

But here's the struggle: many want salvation without sanctification. They want the benefits of the kingdom without the boundaries.

They want freedom from sin, but not freedom from self. But Jesus reminds us: sanctification comes through truth—not trends, not opinions, not emotional highs. It comes through the truth of God's Word and our willingness to "get with the program."

One of the most striking modern examples of someone who *got with the program* was German pastor and theologian Dietrich Bonhoeffer. In the face of Nazi tyranny, Bonhoeffer refused to compromise the truth of the gospel for nationalistic propaganda. While many church leaders folded under the pressure of political allegiance, Bonhoeffer stood firm.

He paid dearly for it, eventually being executed for his resistance. But his life remains a legacy of sanctification in action. He once said, *"When Christ calls a man, he bids him come and die."* Bonhoeffer got with God's program—even when it cost him everything. Why? Because he understood that sanctification through truth isn't just a calling—it's a crucifixion of comfort.

Now, let me clear this up: I am not suggesting you must physically die to "get with the program." But I am saying you will have to *die to self.* To get with the program spiritually means to say yes to God's divine design for your life—even when it disrupts your preferences. It means embracing His truth even when it confronts your comforts and flaws. It means recognizing that the life God calls us to isn't built around convenience—it's shaped by conviction.

Jesus didn't sanctify Himself for applause—He did it for purpose. And He expects us to follow suit. It means surrendering our plans. It means being willing to stand alone. And it means exchanging comfort for calling.

The Apostle Paul echoed this truth when he wrote in Romans 12:1–2: *"Present your bodies a living sacrifice, holy, acceptable unto God… and be not conformed to this world: but be ye transformed by the renewing of your mind."* In a world drowning in half-truths and outright lies, God's truth becomes the anchor that not only transforms but keeps us from drifting. Truth doesn't just inform the mind; it transforms the life. It sets us apart for a higher purpose, making us living witnesses of God's glory.

So what, if anything, is keeping you from getting with the program? Is it a toxic relationship? Is it a lifestyle you won't release? Is it a need for control? Or is it a fear of being different?

True sanctification will always call you out of something and into something greater. Abraham had to leave Ur. Moses had to leave Midian. Ruth had to leave Moab. Jesus left heaven. Why? Because the promise was on the other side of separation.

The truth is many still struggle with embracing truth. Truth is not always convenient. Truth demands surrender. To embrace God's truth is to say "yes" to His will, even when it collides with ours. Truth requires courage. Many walk away from truth because it disrupts the status quo, but to those who embrace it, it brings freedom. *"You shall know the truth, and the truth shall make you free"* (John 8:32).

Truth will confront our flaws, challenge our comfort, and cut through our excuses. And the truth is—compromise delays purpose. As long as you try to hold on to what God told you to release, you're rejecting sanctification. God can't fill hands that won't let go.

The psalmist said in Psalm 119:9, "Wherewithal *shall a young man cleanse his way? By taking heed thereto according to thy word."* Sanctification isn't a one-time act—it's a lifestyle of obedience to the Word. The more you stay in Scripture, the more aligned you become with God's desires.

It is not just about moral cleanliness—it's about mission clarity. God sanctifies you so He can send you. He separates you so He can use you. Jesus modeled it so we could mirror it.

Let's return to our foundational verse: *"For their sakes I sanctify myself, that they also might be sanctified through the truth."* Jesus didn't just model truth—He manifested it. He embodied the discipline, the surrender, and the intentionality of someone fully aligned with divine assignment. And He did it for you.

Now the baton is in our hands. Will we commit to living a consecrated life? Will we let go of what's pulling us away from God's best? Will we let truth disrupt what falsehood tried to decorate?

The call to *get with the program* isn't a call to religion—it's a call to relevance in the kingdom of God. Daniel refused to bow to Babylon's idols because he was anchored in God's truth. His life was set apart for God's glory. John the Baptist spoke truth to power, even when it cost him his life. He lived set apart, pointing people to the Lamb of God.

Jesus prayed, *"For their sakes I sanctify myself, that they also might be sanctified through the truth."* He was declaring that truth was not—and is not—just an idea to be debated; it's a life to be embraced. Truth is the line that sets us apart from the world and sets us apart for God.

When you embrace God's truth, you stop living for your own agenda and start living for His glory. When you embrace God's truth, you no longer conform to the shifting standards of culture but are transformed by the eternal Word of God. When you embrace God's truth, you find the courage to say no to compromise and yes to holiness.

Here's the good news: Jesus didn't just speak truth—He sanctified Himself in truth so that through Him, we can be set apart too. And when truth takes root in your heart, your life becomes a testimony, your witness becomes credible, and your purpose becomes clear.

Because in the end, truth isn't just something we believe. The truth is we follow someone—and His name is Jesus.

LIVING THE LESSON

Throughout the week, take time to put into practice what you've read and reflected on. Each daily activity offers an opportunity to deepen your faith and live out the lessons from this devotional. On the following pages, engage with these activities to grow spiritually and strengthen your relationship with God and others.

Monday | Scripture Focus & Reflection

Begin the week by meditating on what it means to be "sanctified through truth." Reflect on the areas of your life where you are still trying to fit in instead of being set apart.

- John 17:19
- John 8:32
- Romans 12:2
- Leviticus 11:44–45
- 1 Peter 1:15–16

Reflection Questions:

- In what ways are you still trying to fit in instead of standing out for Christ?
- What truth is God revealing to you that challenges your current lifestyle or associations?
- Are you walking in true sanctification or just religious routine?

Journal Prompt:

Write about one area of your life where God is calling you to "get with the program." What changes is He prompting you to make?

_____

_____

_____

_____

_____

_____

_____

_____

_____

Tuesday | Personal Prayer & Petition

Come before God in humility, asking Him to reveal the truth about your current path and empower you to live a life truly set apart.

Prayer Focus:

- Ask God to sanctify you in truth, aligning your life with His Word.
- Pray for clarity about relationships or environments that may be hindering your purpose.
- Ask for strength to release anything that conflicts with God's program for your life.

Journal Prompt:

List the things (e.g. habits, relationships, mindsets) you need to surrender to fully embrace God's program. Turn each into a prayer of release.

_____
_____
_____
_____
_____
_____
_____
_____
_____
_____
_____
_____
_____
_____
_____
_____

Wednesday | Midweek Worship & Gratitude

Worship God for His truth that sets you free. Praise Him for not only calling you out of Egypt but also for giving you purpose and sanctification.

Worship Song Suggestions:

- "Set Apart" – Worship Central
- "Make Room" – Jonathan McReynolds
- "Refiner" – Maverick City Music

Gratitude List:

- Thank God for pulling you out of your "Egypt."
- Thank Him for the Word that sanctifies and transforms you.
- Reflect on how embracing truth has brought you greater freedom and focus.

_____
_____
_____
_____
_____
_____
_____
_____
_____
_____
_____
_____
_____
_____
_____

Thursday | Outreach & Encouragement

Speak truth in love to someone who may be wrestling with compromise. Encourage them to get with God's program and remind them of their worth in Christ.

Outreach Ideas:

- Send a message to a friend encouraging them to embrace their God-given purpose.
- Share a social media post: *"God didn't bring you out of Egypt for you to live like a slave again. Get with the program."*
- Invite someone to a Bible study or devotional group focused on spiritual growth.

Journaling Prompt:

Who has spoken truth into your life at a pivotal moment? Reflect on how you can now be that voice for someone else.

_____

_____

_____

_____

_____

_____

_____

_____

_____

_____

_____

_____

_____

_____

Friday | Self-Examination & Recommitment

Do a spiritual audit. Are there areas where you're half-in and half-out of God's plan? It's time to recommit and fully align with His truth.

Reflection Questions:

- Are you genuinely living set apart, or are you still compromising in some areas?
- What lies have you believed that have kept you from fully embracing God's truth?
- How can you return to a lifestyle of holiness and dedication?

Journal Prompt:

Write a declaration of recommitment to live sanctified in truth. Be specific about what you're releasing and what you're embracing.

_____
_____
_____
_____
_____
_____
_____
_____
_____
_____
_____
_____
_____
_____
_____
_____
_____
_____
_____

Saturday & Sunday | Family Activity & Reflection

Make the weekend a time of reflection and reset for everyone in your household or small group. Focus on truth, sanctification, and setting apart your lives for God's glory.

Group Discussion Ideas:

- Read John 17:19 together and talk about what it means to "get with the program" in modern times.
- Ask: What worldly distractions are trying to pull us off course as a family or group?
- Share what steps you can take together to live more set apart.

Weekend Reflection:

As a family or group, create a "God's Program" commitment list. Have each person write one way they will live more sanctified this week (e.g., time in the Word, breaking off distractions, shifting focus). Post it somewhere visible to encourage accountability.

_____
_____
_____
_____
_____
_____
_____
_____
_____
_____
_____
_____
_____

ACKNOWLEDGMENTS

First and foremost, I would like to express my deepest gratitude *to my wife,* Eugenia, my soulmate and best friend. Your love and support have been my constant source of strength.

To my children—Jamal, Jade, Kevin, and Kahla—you are the air that I breathe. Each of you has inspired me in ways I can never fully express.

To my grandsons and granddaughter—
Jamal Jr., Liyah, Jahlil & Aiyden, Grey, Cyrus, and our newest blessing, Cyan—you are the reason behind everything I have accomplished and achieved. Your presence in my life gives me more joy than words could ever convey.

I would also like to thank *my spiritual leader,* Bishop Orlando Wilson, and my *Manifest Wonders Church family.* Your prayers, fellowship, and encouragement have been instrumental in this journey. I am also grateful for my *iHeartRadio family,* who have been by my side throughout this endeavor.

Finally, a special shout-out to my *industry brothers,* Walt "Baby" Love, Sidney Scott, and Alex Snipes. Your brotherhood has been an irreplaceable part of my life and career, and I am forever thankful for our camaraderie.

Thank you all for walking with me on this journey. You are, without a doubt, my most cherished blessings.

ABOUT THE AUTHOR

Rev. Lee Michaels' life and legacy breathe hope into those who believe their humble beginnings condemn them to a life without promise. After six years of honorable service in the USAF, he shifted from computer management to broadcasting, igniting a passion for radio that propelled him into a successful career, beginning in 1979.

His dedication to radio and community has left an indelible mark on Baltimore, organizing events like the city's first Juneteenth celebration and raising funds for the homeless. Michaels is best known for his 30+ year career at WCAO Heaven 600 AM, where he served as the Morning Show Host and Program Director, earning national acclaim for the station's excellence in gospel music.

Beyond broadcasting, he is the host of the long-running TV show Grace and Glory, an author of the Spiritual Vitamins series, and the founder of Manifest Wonders Church & Performing Arts Center. His commitment to ministry, community service, and entrepreneurship continues to impact countless lives across the Baltimore-Washington region and beyond.

FEATURED PRODUCTS & PROGRAMMING

JOIN LEE MICHAELS

SUNDAYS FROM 1-4PM

for

THIS IS MY STORY

ON

HEAVEN 600, IHEART RADIO

CHECK OUT
YOUTUBE

LEE MICHAELS ATB

DO YOU HAVE THE ENTIRE SET?

Order your copies today!
www.allthingsleemichaels.com

www.ingramcontent.com/pod-product-compliance
Lightning Source LLC
Chambersburg PA
CBHW051149120626
46547CB00012B/1006